ECOCITY BERKELEY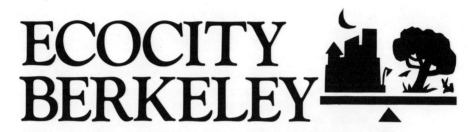

Building Cities for a Healthy Future

The Garden is the paradise of nature,
and the City is the paradise of culture.
Or at least they could be. . . .
Today, both are out of balance.

If we build the ecocity we will regain
the Garden and finally aspire to the full
ideal of the City—the City built with,
not against, nature.

Then, when we hold in reverence that which
we cannot build, which is given to us by
the Earth herself, we will create not just
a home for ourselves but a future for all
who follow.

by RICHARD REGISTER

NORTH ATLANTIC BOOKS, BERKELEY, CALIFORNIA

Published by North Atlantic Books
P.O. Box 12327
Berkeley, California 94712

The illustrations in this book are by the author, with the following exceptions: Cerro Gordo drawings by the Cerro Gordo Town Forum, page 5. Integral Neighborhood, by Bill Mastin, page 23. Slow Street Concept, by Bill Mastin, page 34. Letchworth Plan, from *Garden Cities of Tomorrow* by Ebezener Howard, page 38. Arcosanti, Arizona, 1986, by Paul Okamoto, page 40. Map of Berkeley, Public Works Department, City of Berkeley, California, page 124.

Cover and book design by Paula Morrison
Typeset by Classic Typography

Ecocity Berkeley: Building Cities for a Healthy Future is sponsored by the Society for the Study of Native Arts and Sciences, a nonprofit educational corporation whose goals are to develop an educational and crosscultural perspective linking various scientific, social, and artistic fields; to nurture a holistic view of arts, sciences, humanities, and healing; and to publish and distribute literature on the relationship of mind, body, and nature.

Library of Congress Cataloging-in-Publication Data

Register, Richard, 1943–
    Ecocity Berkeley.

    Bibliography: p.
    1. City planning—California—Berkeley.   2. City planning—Environmental aspects—California—Berkeley.
I. Title.
HT168.B47R45   1987   307.1'2'0979467   86-33215
ISBN 1-55643-009-4

2   3   4   5   6   7   8   9   /   03   02   01   00

ACKNOWLEDGEMENTS

One person far more than any other helped in the preparation of this book. I think it's because, as he told me, "We are carpenters," meaning we build things as well as write and plan. He read, re-read, and sat through hours of friendly debate, made dozens of suggestions and hundreds of corrections of my dreadful spelling because, I think, he'd like to believe books like this help build a healthier, more honest and vital world, one closer to his *Ecotopia* than our present pollution-soaked nuclear time-bomb. Ernest Callenbach, thanks—I'm very grateful.

Many of the ideas here are my own, but equally as many were generated by my fellow members of Urban Ecology during the decade of the organization's activity, from 1975 to 1985. Special thanks to Rus Adams, Joe Alcamo, Sue Stropes, Gary Farber, Stuart Chaitkin, John Coveney, Elyce Judith, Casey Morrigan, and Walter Truette Anderson for years of working together, developing and refining these ideas. In 1986 the big contributors to our last projects and this book in particular were Judith Goldsmith, Bill Mastin and Ariel Rubissow. And a special thanks to Richard Grossinger of North Atlantic Books, a publishing partner long awaited and much appreciated.

, In later printings I hope I'll be able to list those friends in Berkeley City government and in local organizations (and in other cities) who set out upon the path of rebuilding their town. I'll say, "Thanks on behalf of all us citizens who are simply in love with the new Berkeley, on behalf of all those salmon in the creeks; those healthy, happy fruit trees; the children who get a kick out of the fluttering wind mills and sparkling greenhouses; thanks for making our town into an ecocity, thanks after all those Reagan years with no vision for a future at all, for helping us to dream again and learn how to build our dreams."

TABLE OF CONTENTS

INTRODUCTION

The purpose of this book is to present the concept of ecocities, to suggest ways for people to take part in transforming their existing towns and cities into ecocities, and to propose changes in one particular city, Berkeley, California. The section on Berkeley illustrates the ideas with concrete examples of changes in planning, architecture, policy, and citizen action; it could—and *should*—be rewritten for any and all other cities, similarly in principle, but differently according to each city's special circumstances.

This book is about changes, basic and big. It seeks to open our minds to broader and more long-range perspectives than embodied in building and planning as usual. It proposes moving towards vital, healthy, challenging, creative cities. Such changes will never be easy or even always comfortable. Without a certain amount of stress and strenuous exercise, neither the individual's body nor mind grows in health or wisdom. So too with the city. And stress and exercise will have to take place at the deepest levels: we can no longer afford simply to accept whatever technology makes available and build and pursue lifestyles without regard to underlying values, without concern for repercussions into the deep future. The choices we face in deciding how to build our cities have a profound influence on the future health of the Earth and all life on it, so many are we who live in cities, so far-ranging is the effect of the way we build and live.

We of the so-called developed and developing worlds are at a point of crisis in the way we live. We are destroying our planet's life systems at the rate of one species or more every hour and we are exhausting its resources at a devastating rate—in the case of fossil fuels, at 1,000,000 years of natural geologic accumulation every year.

In this situation, immediate action needs to be viewed in the context of long-range goals and overall vision. In this situation we must be open to ideas that may seem strange at first, that might come from unexpected quarters, that don't necessarily fit any of the mainstream or alternative orthodoxies. *Ecocities seek the health and vitality of humanity and nature, and that is all. And, that is enough—because it can guide all the rest.*

What is proposed here is a tentative but fairly rigorous set of principles and proposed actions that fit these goals. This book is not the final word on the subject, but a kind of position statement designed to open the subject to public debate. You will find general concepts here that every person who lives in a town or city should be aware of and ultimately capable of dealing with. You will find forthright and practical suggestions about what the author thinks should be done. And, if you are inclined to action, you are provided with publications and organizations in the resources guides at the end of the book.

Finally, a word of caution about building ecocities in this world of debilitating limits and catastrophic dangers that we have created for ourselves, a word that will make all the difference: have fun!

Part 1

ECOCITY...

WHAT IS AN ECOCITY?

An ecocity is an ecologically healthy city. No such city exists. There are bits and pieces of the ecocity scattered about in present-day cities and sprinkled through history, but the concept—and hopefully, the reality—is just beginning to germinate.

In the old European cities and towns and in the pueblos of the Indians of the American Southwest we see hints of the ecocity: these were compact, lively settlements that wasted little land and consumed little energy. Using local building materials and changing only slowly over many generations, these towns weathered into the landscape and aesthetically merged with the natural rhythms. Of course, there was no real smog and no toxic or radiological waste until recent times, though some towns exhausted their resources: the pueblo of Mesa Verde, in southern Colorado, stripped most of the trees right off the landscape for miles around for firewood—and water contamination from human and animal waste was, literally, a plague upon Medieval European cities.

We see hints of the ecocity in today's solar, wind, and recycling technologies. In creek restoration projects, urban gardening and fruit tree planting, we see more signs of movement in that direction. In individuals using foot, bike and public modes of transportation in preference to the automobile, we get another glimpse of a radically different future. In concern about resource depletion, pollution, over-population and extinction of species, we have a necessary precondition for ecocities: people caring about the future and in many cases, working for it.

Several organizations have been working for ten to twenty years to build prototypes of ecologically healthy towns and cities. Arcosanti,

Turrette-sur-Loup, France—distinct town/country boundary

Below: Compact city of canyons and bridges in a canyon with access by train and foot. Greenhouses and agriculture on one quarter, forest surrounding.

Arizona, and Cerro Gordo, Oregon, are both start-from-scratch "new towns" that began building on unoccupied land. There have also been efforts to reshape existing cities—by Urban Ecology in Berkeley, California, and Citizen Planners in Los Angeles.

But the truth is, that despite a few positive signs and efforts, we are sliding backward much faster than forward at this point. Such projects will have to begin happening simultaneously and in much larger numbers if ecocities are to be built. Most important, the concept must be firmly established and broadly understood and supported. Then, not only will we create the "sustainable" city that coexists peacefully with nature, but we will also discover a new creative adventure accessible to everyone, and, ultimately, nothing less than a new mode of existence and creative fulfillment on this planet.

Left: Paolo Soleri's concept of a city in a single large structure, which he calls "arcology."

Below: Convivial, "human-scale" courtyard—an ideal to Cerro Gordo planners.

Cluster housing planned for Cerro Gordo, Oregon.

THE PRESENT SITUATION—
CITY, NATURE, AND THE CHIEF
AGENT OF THEIR DEMISE

Something almost magic comes from cross-fertilization of ideas, ambitions, and basic human sociability when people gather in cities to share and take advantage of the gifts of others. Problems arise too, but what is unique in an individual and useful to society is served by the city in ways that would be impossible without it. The city is a rich soil in which ideas, art, science, and innovation grow. It is a human social invention that makes other inventions possible.

Many have said that the city is the physical container of culture and civilization. Some have said that, without the city, culture and civilization could have never come into being. Jane Jacobs, in *Cities and the Wealth of Nations*, has suggested that the city, integrated successfully with its immediate hinterlands, is the very engine of prosperity, the basic economic unit of culturally diverse society. Jacobs goes so far as to present examples of cities that revitalize nature in areas once over-exploited by rural people—while at the same time bringing new prosperity to the rural people themselves.

In the last decade the practitioners of bioregionalism have pointed out the value of learning about the place in which you live: the geology, climate, weather, soils, animal and plant populations, and the full history of human interrelations with them. Bioregional thinking has rekindled the value of sense of place and has alerted people to the extent of their impacts on nature. You can't miss what you never knew. But by teaching us about the full richness of our biological environments, bioregionalists make it possible for people to know what they have had the misfortune never to have experienced personally, to miss it, want it back, and to become empowered to get it back.

Cities, we learn from ecocity studies, could be rebuilt to fit gracefully,

---

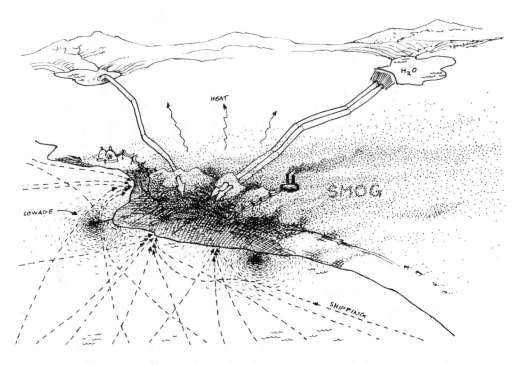

SPRAWLED FLAT CITY WITH SUPPLY LINES AND POLLUTION.

non-destructively, even regeneratively into their bioregions. They could become instruments accomplishing two priceless goals: 1.) fuller creative evolution of society and the individual, and 2.) healthy coevolution and mutual support with nature.

Ecocities could replace the type of growth that presently prevails— wasteful, ecologically unhealthy sprawl—by a development implicitly aware of its limits. A healthy future requires *change* and *a different kind of growth*, with some cities shrinking, becoming much more compact and far less sprawled, some breaking up into smaller units while local population stays the same or increases, some taking responsibility for regional population growth while publicizing the need for lower birth rates and decreasing human impact on nature. The particular kinds of growth and change which could turn today's cities into ecocities depends on the bioregion of each city and the imagination of its citizens.

Without question the most destructive agent of social disintegration, ecological contamination, poisoning of people and environment, waste of energy, and even homicide (outstripping violent crime by more than two to one) is the automobile. Or, more accurately, it is the inter-

---

relation of automobiles and sprawled, generally single-use and low-density land-use patterns: Auto Sprawl Syndrome. Auto Sprawl Syndrome is not only killing a good many of us, while poisoning the rest and suffocating 3 million new acres of land a year in the United States under asphalt and concrete (says the American Farmland Trust), it has also hood-winked us—in a big way! We think the car is "fast," helps us zip around and get a lot done quickly. But if we add to the time we are speeding along, the time we are stuck in traffic jams, looking for parking places, waiting for repairs, cleaning and polishing, paying or contesting tickets at the courthouse, visiting victims in hospitals and funerals, recovering from accidents ourselves, and working to pay for the car, it's *a lot of time*! Divide the miles the average person drives in a year by that amount of time and you get 5 to 7 miles per hour! (Ivan Illich makes these calculations citing national statistics in his book *Energy and Equity*.) We are conditioned to think the street-and-road-system is cost-effective and auto-drivers are paying their way while bus and train passengers are openly subsidized, freeloading on the public treasury and good will. Vice versa, I'm afraid. There are countless hidden, unacknowledged, and embarrassing subsidies to the automobile, including tax losses for land used for streets, highways, widening of streets, and for freeway interchanges. Other massive subsidies include free traffic control services (police), highway lighting, signs and signals, subsidies to car-dependent suburban sprawl for cheap water, new electric service, schools, etc., subsidies in banking practices that provide investment opportunities to sprawl developers while withholding loans to in-town (especially small-scale) non-auto oriented projects—not to speak of costs caused by car drivers but paid by everybody: emphysema and lung cancer bills, the price of repainting houses eroded by pollution, repairing public monuments etched away by airborne acids and losses to the fishing industry due to street runoff and acid rain.

Look a little deeper and you discover that Auto Sprawl Syndrome is subsidized so generously that transit subsidies look minuscule in comparison.

But you can't just eliminate the car. How would suburbanites get to work? The car is part of a syndrome or system. Cars make sprawl possible. Once built, people living in the sprawl pattern are completely dependent on the individual vehicle. Some people say they don't like their job but have to keep it to pay for the car because if they didn't have a car they couldn't get to work. Most suburbanites are too thinly scattered to use trains, even too thinly scattered for effective bus service.

But if Auto Sprawl Syndrome is hard on commuters and degrades the environment for all of us, the impact is small today compared to what we can expect in the near future. The larger effects of the way we build cities and live in them may be difficult to see from our perspective in history. Walter Truett Anderson, environmentalist and political scientist (*To Govern Evolution*, 1987) believes the link between today's cities and global climate change and damage to the biosphere is clearly established and that in the next few years awareness of these issues will have to grow rapidly—and of necessity, will. Says Anderson, "When historians of the future look back on 1986, they may well conclude that the biggest news story of the year was the one that barely made it onto the front page: a sudden increase in global concern about the 'greenhouse effect.'"

A closely related development: in 1986 a hole in the ozone layer was discovered over Antarctica. It appears to be widening rapidly—a forewarning of widespread increase in cancer, many scientists believe. "Unless the current scientific consensus proves to be dead wrong," writes Anderson, "the world will be thrust into dealing with a global issue every bit as urgent as nuclear war, one that literally affects every living thing on the planet and that cannot with ease be postponed."

Lester Brown of the World Watch Institute of Washington, D.C. has proposed a "CO_2-benign" strategy to develop energy conserving and renewable (sun, wind, water) energy technology. When more people realize that cities could be restructured to radically reduce energy consumption while providing an appropriate context for "appropriate technologies"—and serve a dozen other healthy purposes to boot, *then* we will be thinking on a scale to save the atmosphere, conserve the ozone layer and prevent the ecological destruction of most of Earth's life systems.

The fact is, if we want to leave any energy reserves and a reasonably healthy biosphere to our children, we will need to change *the whole system* so that cars are no longer an integral part. We will, in other words, have to completely rebuild our cities on ecocity lines.

FIRST THINGS FIRST—
DEAL WITH THE CAUSES

One of the most important axioms of ecology is that all things are connected in a complex web of relationships. Some connections are very direct, some very indirect. Some causes have conspicuous and immediate effects. Some cause and effect chains are very long, and often, important causes are far from conspicuous. Sometimes a key factor that causes a problem is hidden deep in a chain of events, and so, to solve the problem might require an effort to trace that chain back to particularly important "root" causes. For instance, some would put smog devices on cars to control the symptoms of air pollution, but others would perceive the more basic need to get out of their cars and take transit or ride bikes. At a deeper level of cause and effect, it becomes apparent that even decent transit has trouble connecting the scattered city—the city itself needs to be restructured so that more is available closer together with less need to move about, less required investment in transportation, less cost in wasted time, less expense in attempting to clean up. Since all things are connected (if often very subtly), getting back to deeper causes provides linked solutions to multiple problems: restructuring for diversity at close proximity makes restoration of natural habitat and regeneration of local species possible and helps create cultural variety.

The Office of Technology Assessment, a research arm of the United States Congress, provides us with a cogent example of what happens when there is little interest in the causes of problems. One of the Office's recent reports asserted that less than 1 percent of the nation's $70 billion anti-pollution effort is aimed at curbing production of wastes, and current programs do "little more than move wastes around."

Seeking changes at the level of causes is not the habit of politics, which moves from crisis to reaction to patch-up—and when it gets really bad—to cover-up. Seeking changes at the level of causes is not the habit of planning either, which ironically, is also indifferent to the long-term effects of plans as well: the long-term future has no living, voting constituents, and doesn't pay the planners' fees and salaries.

But dealing with changes at the level of causes is necessary if cities are to become vital, healthy, enduring creations.

PRINCIPLES OF ECOCITY-BUILDING

CRITERIA: LIFE, BEAUTY, EQUITY

At the foundation of all that follows in this book are the *reasons* for building in the ways suggested. It is in the service of defending, exploring, and cherishing life on Earth that ecocities will be built. If cities are built for maximum profit for the powerful and financially clever, or to confer maximum material wealth on all citizens equally, or to find some midpoint on the materialistic continuum between those extremes, the ecocity will wither at its inception. Nonetheless, making a living and seeking personal material security are major motivations to all of us who live in and help to build and run cities. So both kinds of reasons—those that provide a healthy, adventuresome, beautiful environment, and those that support the needs and desires of the individual, singly and collectively—must be accommodated.

The aesthetic of a city—its sensitivity and style, the way its buildings, streets, and transportation systems are constructed, its relation to its natural and designed biological environment, its many ways of functioning—is of great importance. As the Navajos attempt to "walk in beauty," so too urban citizens should discover in themselves ways to build and live in beauty.

And there needs to be "equity": fairness among people, the full opportunity for citizens to choose, create, and live out their own special expressions of potential. The city is an instrument for human purpose—without this equity it fails in its human purpose whether it impacts negatively or positively upon nature.

There should be nothing strange, embarrassing, or egotistical about attempting to enhance life, beauty, and equity. It is simple considera-

tion for others on a large but finite planet. It is the kind of citizenship already widely accepted as a goal, if seldom attained.

BIOREGION, BIOLOGY AND THE CITY

We can draw the borders of a bioregion according to types of living species, watersheds, winds, air drainages, geographic and geological features, and climates. But seldom is a natural border as distinct as the one between a tidal pool blossoming with multi-colored life, and, just above the high tide mark, a desert with a few scattered cacti per acre and a few scattered showers per year. And yet, some creatures, birds for example, often ply the two zones on either side of the natural border and consider them both as aspects of one place called home. Nothing crisp or dogmatic exists to help us map bioregions, yet it is

DIVERSITY: There are the same number of natural species in the pictures on p. 14 and p. 15, but in p. 15 picture, people and many useful species are added. There might be somewhat smaller *populations* of each natural species, but the number of *species* remains the same. This would be the highest goal possible for long-range health of the biosphere: human and natural coevolutionary diversity.

in this very reality of differences from one place to another that we find the richness and value of unique local offerings—those special events and potentials that are fascinating to the naturalist, raw material for the inventor, subject for the artist and poet, most simply our source of "reverence for life."

Since we late twentieth-century city-dwellers are more familiar with our technologies and cities than we are with the natural elements of our bioregion and biosphere, and since what we build often stands between us and nature, like the hundreds of square miles of suburbia surrounding almost all present-day cities, it is especially urgent to learn as much as we can from nature. We need to touch nature more intimately, let our children grow up knowing that vegetables don't just appear in the supermarket by magic, knowing instead the magic of sun, wind, rain, creeks, bees, butterflies, flowers, gardens, farms. . . .

This biological aspect of the ecocity is what some have called the "Green City." Fundamental biological principles apply to the greening of cities.

- *Diversity is healthy* (see drawings, p. 14 and p. 15). The number of species and variety of habitats and resources in an area, and the complexity of their interconnections are generally measures of ecological stability and, if disturbed, resilience.
- *Fairly large areas are required for natural species to develop diversity of population.* Generally, people should create settlements that, on a map, look something like "spots" against a background of natural and agricultural land, rather than sprawl that becomes a background against which parks and natural areas look like spots.

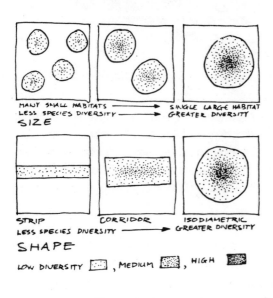

Principles of biogeography applied to design of wildlife habitat (left), and applied to ecocity design (right).

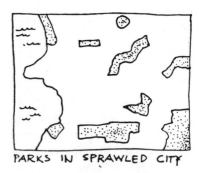

PARKS IN SPRAWLED CITY

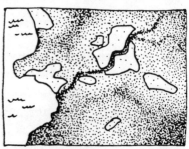

COMPACT ECOCITIES IN NATURE (SAME LOCATION)

- *Land has a limit to the quantity of biological material it can naturally support in a particular climate, called its "carrying capacity."* Given the climate and soils of an environment, the resident plants and animals can extract only so much water, minerals, and energy in creating their bodies, the collective "biomass." Another limit to carrying capacity is the rate at which the total population can reprocess that biological material into usable biological resources through decomposition and soil building.

    It is easy for people to thoughtlessly reduce an environment's carrying capacity—to strip its forests or pollute it with poisons. The diverse bioregion then collapses, regenerating over hundreds, even thousands of years (if ever). It's far more difficult to increase long-term carrying capacity. Sustained composting, rebuilding of soil, solar desalinization and supply of water, and planting trees can provide the resources that invite and sustain populations of different species. However, many species simply are not compatible with people and their present habits. The capacity of the environment to support these species can be completely destroyed by a few roads and periodic killing and carting off of plants and animals for food, building materials, or hobby and sport. The California condor, now facing extinction, is a case in point: with the intrusion of even a small number of hunters and with the loss of available carrion, the habitat has lost its carrying capacity as far as this stately, soaring giant is concerned.

- *There is a green hierarchy in ecocity planting.* Natural (native) and useful (food, medicinal, wood-providing) plants are much more important for ecological and social health than ornamentals, though this rule is softened by the diversity principle. Lawns presently consume vast areas, waste water, energy, and time, and tempt people to apply expensive fertilizers and dangerous pesticides. Why not plant food gardens, ground covers of herbs and strawberries, fruit and nut trees?

- *Make wastes into new resources:* compost and recycle.

- *Biological pest control and nutrients are generally preferable to chemicals.* Use parasitic wasps to control aphids and natural manure and compost in gardening, for example.

- *When it comes to extinction and diminution of species, urbanites, suburbanites, and rural people all conspire,* if only half-consciously. Cities, per se, are not the cause of this problem. Fences, country roads, range and forest management, replacement of natural species with useful ones (cattle, for example), deforestation for agriculture, flooding valleys to benefit city and farm alike for electricity and water, living far from work and commuting . . . , all these can intrude severely on natural species.

Biological principles suggest many ways to help build ecocities. We can preserve or restore creeks, rivers, shorefronts, marshes, and springs whenever possible, and build structures either at a respectful distance or in an appreciative, enhancing relationship to the water. We can prevent excess runoff from damaging creeks, bays, and wetlands by collecting water in cisterns and sumps or by using "permeable paving," and narrower sidewalks and streets. We can avoid contamination of what inevitably does run off by reducing the number of cars, acreage of parking lots, new and used car lots, and the like; size and number of gas stations; and by not drenching lawns and golf courses in insecticides, herbicides, and chemical fertilizers. The number of dogs as well as cars in the city can be reduced—the waste products of both kill aquatic life when swept into the waterways via storm drains. If kids splash in the water and mud (safely) they learn to love (and respect) it.

More gardening—urban orchards, solar greenhouses, rooftop gardens—is important for ecocities. We can bring agricultural areas up to the "gates of the city," that is, virtually into places where large numbers of people live and work, making serious food-raising a conscious part of every urban person's experience. This can be accomplished by gradually withdrawing from thinly populated auto-dependent areas, establishing gardens and orchards in parks and along streets, hiring urban farmers and, providing agricultural services and tax breaks.

We can re-establish or permit natural life forms to coexist with the city by giving them sizable slices of their natural habitat around the city (greenbelt instead of suburbia), and within it (in parks, along restored creeks and shorelines). These border zones (forest/meadow, water/land, etc.) are among the most diverse and ecologically valuable parts of the natural habitat. Public and private funds should be established to gradually buy and remove badly located buildings. At the same time, *more* space serving the same uses (housing, work, education—whatever uses that are displaced) should be built in ecologically preferable locations in the same town. Zoning and tax incentives can assist in opening up the city to nature while shifting urban activity to other, more focused and diverse areas. Individuals can provide habitat and food for birds and bees by planting appropriately, providing beehives, or allowing natural hives in the parks and along creeks, with a buffer zone (you only need about 30 feet) between hives and houses. Reducing the number of cars and slowing their speed will reduce the deaths of opposum, deer, squirrels, frogs, and turtles—as well as of dogs, cats, cyclists, and pedestrians—and avoid driving animals away with unpleasant noise.

We can also clean and recycle. The importance of reducing air, water, chemical, and radiological contamination is fortunately becoming widely recognized; soon we may even get back to root causes here, too, and substantially curtail making and buying un-recyclable and contaminating products in the first place.

THE SHAPE OF THINGS TO COME— THREE-DIMENSIONAL, NOT FLAT

If we don't want to steal the fossil fuels from our children (and there are many better uses for oil than burning), if we want to leave them a legacy of vital cities and a healthy environment, we need to build cities in a far more compact manner than is prevalent today. Even farm houses in the country which in America are scattered widely over a lonely landscape, would serve social and ecological goals better if clustered into compact villages and small towns. Some European "farm houses" are little more than tool sheds with beds; the farmers often live in town where they have their social life close at hand and walk or ride out to the farm for work, staying over as the seasonal work demands, and occasionally on weekends or holidays for a change of pace.

Cities, instead of being flat like a tortilla, should be three-dimensional—much more like the old cities of Europe, though not necessarily as three-dimensional as Manhattan. And they can't, without great environmental damage, be narrow-mindedly dense like downtown San Francisco, which is almost exclusively work space, and one specific kind at that: office work.

Higher densities must be combined with mixed uses. Instituting mixed-use zoning and zoning that concentrates development rather than scattering it is an important part of the solution. Requiring developers to build apartments in or near tall buildings is helpful. Constructing buildings, even very large ones, with a smaller grain or texture, that is, broken up into different parts and shapes instead of constructing them as simple giant boxes, also contributes to urban diversity and

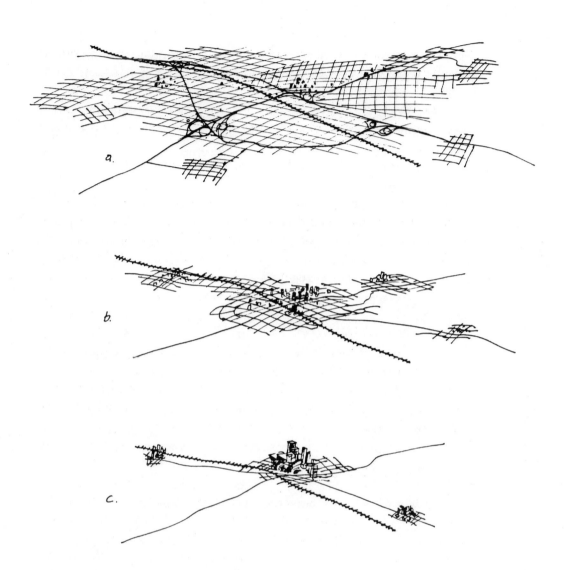

FLAT CITIES—COMPACT CITIES

vitality.

Diversity, which is healthy in ecological systems, is also healthy for society and economy in cities. If sprawl is destructive for forcing people to live in large expanses of uniform use and forcing people to travel long distances in polluting, energy-wasting vehicles, then so is the dense single-use downtown at the other end of the commute. The solution is to increase diversity as new development replaces or supplements old.

Many actions support diverse three-dimensionality. We can adopt "proximity policies" that prescribe hiring, renting, and loaning preferentially to people working close to home and people who don't own cars.

We can tax cars, dividing the Blue Book value by miles per gallon times a constant would favor lower-income and lower-energy-consuming car-owners.

Individuals can do their best to move closer to work or find work closer to home.

City plans can set quotas for new development and guide the citizenry toward balanced diversity. For example, if a downtown and its immediate neighborhood are composed of 90% work space and 10% housing, future building could be, say, 30% work space and 70% housing until a better balance is reached and commuting radically reduced. This can be legally regulated in new zoning and by ordinance. It can be promoted by tax penalties on one hand or tax reduction or forgiveness on the other.

Just to *imagine* development in "spots" or small areas of great diversity is very helpful, large downtown spots and smaller ones in smaller neighborhood centers. Public transportation works best when moving people from one active spot to another; it doesn't work well attempting to connect scattered low-density sprawl.

NEIGHBORHOODS

Even if downtowns and adjacent neighborhoods are far more attractive, pleasant, and healthy, many people will want to live in lower density areas; *how* low, *how* scattered, and *how* uniform is the critical issue. It's a matter of degree, of not "going too far," in this case toward the uniform suburban sprawl that characterizes development patterns today. Generally, the following would be helpful steps moving the city toward ecological health.

- *Preserve medium density neighborhoods while vitalizing their centers*, adding population within two or three blocks of these centers. Bring back the corner store and add a few apartments upstairs. Add housing space near the centers by encouraging garage, basement, and attic conversions into bedrooms or complete living units, or by raising the house and adding a story.
- *Withdraw from low density neighborhoods and areas of medium density in sensitive or rich ecological areas* such as creeks and shorelines, steep

---

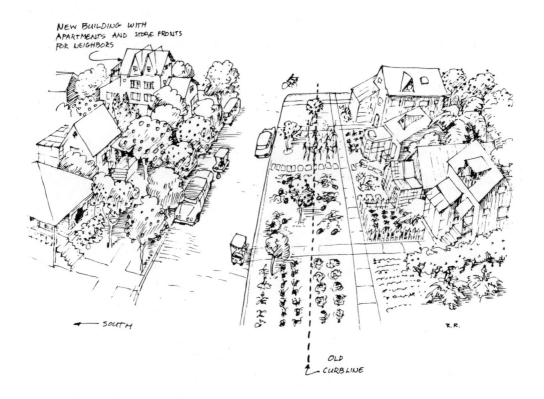

NEW BUILDING WITH
APARTMENTS AND STORE FRONTS
FOR NEIGHBORS

SOUTH

R.R.

OLD
CURBLINE

REDUCING STREET WIDTH: Making neighborhood streets narrower—
we're not talking about arterials or transit corridors here—should be done
in neighborhoods that are medium density. Design to allow emergency vehicle
access is important and legal impediments can be significant, but if enough
people would like to do it, it can be done. Just demand that the common
practice of widening streets be put into reverse.

In this illustration, yard space for gardening is added to the yards of the
houses on the sunny (north) side of the street, driveways replaced with berry
patches and vegetable gardens, small fruit trees spaced sparsely so that the
yards remain free of large shadow areas.

The south side of the street, shaded largely by the houses, is a good location for larger fruit and nut trees. Since in the ecocity general plan for this
town this particular neighborhood is slated for slightly higher density, several
apartments and shops for neighborhood services have been added to the new
building on the corner (top left). Greenhouses appear on the south sides of
most homes. Very low auto traffic volume means vegetables can be grown
in front yards without accumulating lead, asbestos, rubber dust, etc., and it
means healthy, safe biking and jogging.

INTEGRAL NEIGHBORHOOD: This "integral neighborhood" is a very diverse "mixed use" area. It's integral in the sense that its various functions are closely linked and usefully related one to another. Homes, jobs, schools, recreation, natural features (like the open creek) and agricultural features (like the many gardens and fruit trees) make the neighborhood a kind of village in the city. The basics of a lively community are all here—and so is the culture of the city and all its special contributions that require a larger population base: nearby downtown, schools of higher learning, theaters, research centers, hospitals. . . . In the integral neighborhood there is some animal raising, almost complete recycling, solar and wind energy harnessed, fuel energy conserved with insulation and non-auto transportation. Some professional offices and arts, crafts and trades work spaces fit well here. There's opportunity in nooks and crannies and on specially designed rooftops for childcare, play areas, cafes, places to simply sit and watch the views, people, birds, creek. . . .

---

slopes, beautiful rock outcroppings, and special views that should be available to any citizen.
- *In very large suburban sprawls, locate good potential centers and begin focusing development there while withdrawing from areas at greater distance from the centers.* Either that or if the whole area has little reason for being other than as a bedroom to a city, then general withdrawal should be initiated.
- *Make most streets narrower while adding garden space.*
- *Use positive incentives* when withdrawing development in one place and increasing it in another. Public and private funds (reprioritized tax money, bond money, endowments, land banking, non-profit donations, etc.) and other kinds of assistance should be available to more than compensate people for moving. Transfer of development rights from low density areas to higher density areas could be worked out to help developers build in the right places.

Many neighborhood changes can be initiated by individuals acting alone or in small groups. Establishing a garden or building a solar greenhouse is nothing out of the ordinary; information is available from gardeners, designers and construction tradespeople, and in many books.

When it comes to increasing or decreasing densities, broader efforts are required, zoning needs to be changed along with tax incentives, city services, streets, and more. Neighborhoods tend to be extremely conservative, so it's important to approach the city government first with the whole city in mind.

TALL BUILDINGS, HIGH DENSITY

Height limits are often imposed as an anti-development strategy, and usually because tall buildings are seen as causing traffic congestion. Insofar as height limits show an appreciation of limits in general and take into account the qualitative changes that accompany quantitative changes, they are well motivated, meaningful, and sometimes beneficial; they put the brakes on run-away single-use construction.

But since the idea behind ecocities is not to stop development nor reverse the clock but to move into the future by encouraging particular kinds of development, height limits have to be reconsidered in another light.

On the negative side, tall buildings cast long shadows, make streets cooler, often increase winds especially on wide streets, add lots of people

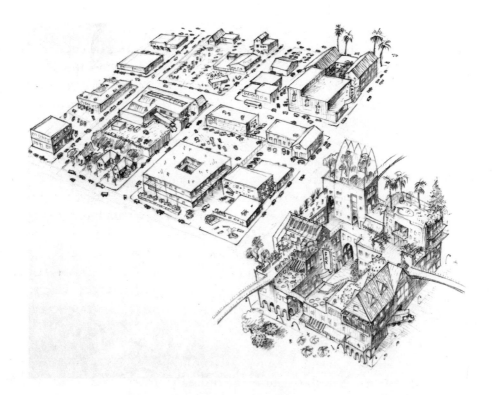

FLAT VS. COMPACT DEVELOPMENT

Thirty to sixty percent of most American cities are given over mainly to the automobile. Many urban activities, such as theater, warehousing, photo lab work and certain industrial processes don't need much natural lighting—or even require artificial lighting only. These activities can be placed underneath other more sun-loving uses. The compact single block pictured here represents all the buildings featured in the more sprawled five block area, but rearranged. If the car is eliminated from the five block area, the land required for the same activities would be reduced to about two and a half blocks. And if less light-dependent activities are housed under the others, the area required would be reduced about half again.

In both drawings there is a hotel, movie theater, bar, three restaurants, two cafes, one warehouse, one photo lab, a dozen small shops including a small grocery, fifteen offices and 120 units of housing. What the sprawl has that the three-dimensional block doesn't have: parking, a gas station and three small houses. What the compact block has that the sprawl doesn't have: two rooftop greenhouses, twice as many trees and bushes, outdoor cafes, great views from the third floor up, foot bridges connecting with other blocks on the fourth floor level, and four blocks of land liberated for nature, agriculture or recreation. The compact block is also much quieter, has no smog and, on the average night, has ten times as many stars overhead in the clear, almost glare-free sky.

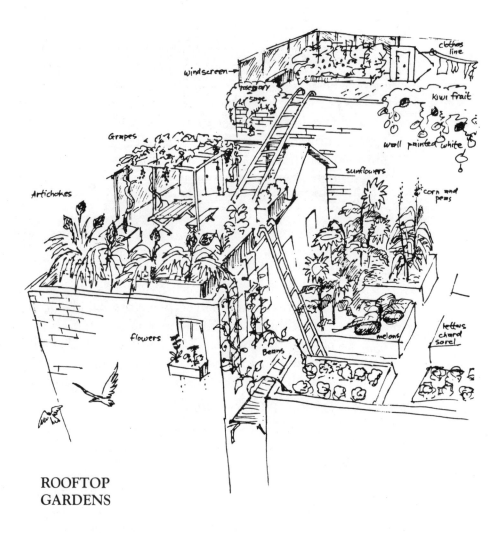

Labels on illustration: clothes line, windscreen, rosemary, sage, kiwi fruit, Grapes, wall painted white, sunflowers, Artichokes, corn and peas, flowers, melons, lettuce chard sorel, Beans

**ROOFTOP
GARDENS**

to an area, can appear alienating and ugly—and, in today's development patterns, usually *do* clog the streets with new traffic.

But when you look more closely at these negatives, they become more conditional, less absolute. A windswept bluff overlooking ocean swells and exploding surf can be an inspiring place for many people—but few enjoy a wind trying to sweep them down a city street. Many people enjoy shady forests and the subtle light that filters through spanish moss and ferns in deep canyons—but not as many appreciate cool streets with the sun glinting back and forth between glass curtain walls (unless it is a hot summer day).

But what if some people *like* to live among or near tall buildings and like the lifestyles and the cultural variety that larger numbers of people make possible? (Millions do.) What if instead of dreary repetition of giant boxes and filing cabinets we had beautiful buildings. (Some exist.) Why not develop according to mixed-use guidelines and proximity policies as suggested earlier? Then tall buildings would not cause tense, noisy, smelly, dangerous streets because cars would seldom be needed and could then be barred altogether from large areas of town, creating, as Ernest Callenbach called them in *Ecotopia*, "carfree zones." And would it not be possible to create intimate, personal, even cozy spaces daringly sited 20 stories up in a sunny nook in a cluster of tall buildings? This is a new kind of border zone scarcely experimented with as yet, the border between the subtle and the spectacular, the small and the large, the secure and the exciting, the immediate, personal scale, and the scale revealed by a high-flying view of much of the bioregion.

Tall buildings and dense downtowns are not a cut-and-dried negative like smog or toxic waste, abject poverty or epidemic disease. In fact, in the right context and built and functioning in an ecologically well-tuned manner, heights and densities of a relatively high level are part of the solution to a long list of problems. On the positive side, construction of tall buildings and dense, diverse downtowns, compared to low-density, uniform development:

- saves vast acreage of land for agriculture and nature,
- promotes energy saving, non- or low-polluting pedestrian, bicycle, and transit access,
- makes commerce and culture and social diversity of all kinds easily available, and,
- can be built with multi-leveled solar greenhouses, rooftop gardens, fruit trees in the streets, restored creeks, and with other elements of biology extending into and through the city.

It should be remembered, too, that different people have different needs and interests, different work and lifestyles, many of which could be ecologically healthy. A family's needs are different from a single person's. A young student may enjoy a different living arrangement from that same person in retirement fifty years later. Any discussion of height limits and densities needs to take two basic things into consideration: the diversity of the culture and the health of the biosphere. All other categories are not imperative.

To promote the right kinds of tall buildings and oppose the wrong kinds, the strategy is fairly straightforward.

Note whether they add or subtract from diversity of an area,

A POSSIBILITY FOR A LARGE CITY DOWNTOWN: A possibility for a large city downtown. This one is a take-off on San Francisco, with some of its buildings modified, some missing, some added. Key features: forest of giant redwoods, near left, and bridges, fruit trees, creeks, taxis and buses but no private automobiles. Though still mainly commercial, this downtown houses many more people than the present downtown San Francisco, and virtually all the workers who don't live here come in on short commutes by bus, train, and bike. Some of the buildings are imagined to have been built before ecocity ideas were adopted and later retro-fitted (the building with hexagonal floor plan, left of center) and some are designed from scratch to take advantage of sun angles (the building immediately in front of the one just mentioned).

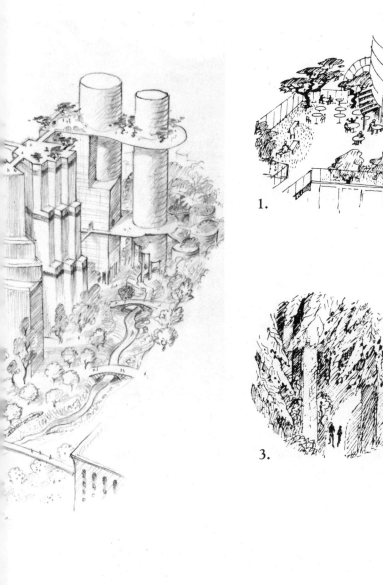

ZOOMING IN ON DOWNTOWN

1. South-facing rooftop cafe: wind-screened, cozy, yet spectacular views.
2. Urban-alpine needle: wild wind, dangerous feeling, exciting.
3. Downtown forest: cool, very quiet.
4. Everyday street corner scene plus more trees, buses, benches, residents.
5. Wind-screened rooftop tennis and orchard.

These scenes are blow-ups from the drawing on the facing page and illustrate the many kinds of environments that are possible in downtowns.

whether they overwhelm or fit into a particular location, and whether or not they are attractive. The appropriateness to a particular area and the aesthetic question are much more subjective than the impact on diversity and commuting, but in all cases, anyone can have an opinion and . . .

. . . express it in any way available. To protest a building or a higher density area as inappropriate is of only meager use once it is built. Refusing to patronize shops in an offending building or area might have some influence on future development, but it's far better to put up resistance long before the project is built. Speaking at hearings, writing letters, and organizing other people can all be effective—sometimes startlingly effective. Small local groups, and occasionally a single individual, can transform a hundred thousand square feet of office space into a hundred living units, or require that a developer restore a creek, relocate a whole cluster of buildings from a car-dependent area to a transit hub, or establish a new bus-route. It happens all the time! And it can have profound influence on the not-so-distant future.

The creative approach that advocates better ways to build can piggy-back on any hearing: "why not build this instead of that . . . ," followed by suggestions. At present many of the more novel ideas for making high densities liveable, even exciting, seem impractical, unrealistic, "visionary". But it's amazing how realistic things become when a lot of people and key decision-makers start talking about them. Footbridges between buildings, rooftop gardens—even ponds—several stories up are not only possible but have been built. Kaiser Center in Oakland, California, for example, has all of these features and it would be difficult to get away with calling Kaiser Aluminum and Steel impractical. So always start by asking for what you'd *really* like to see, with full biological diversity, energy conservation, usefulness, and sustainability for your children's sake—all those healthy, enjoyable, idealistic things— and *then* compromise as necessary. The vision has to come before submersion in the inevitable practical details, just as the working drawings have to precede pouring the concrete and ordering the 2x4s and nails.

When it comes to influencing what gets built in higher density areas, the most effective two places to apply personal energy are in educating people about positive approaches and in taking part in early planning. This includes dealing with zoning, master plans, long public hearings, and wrangling with the bureaucracy. People who are shy about public speaking or find it difficult to lobby City Council members or

to approach bureaucracy may find talking to one person at a time, writing a letter to an editor, or supporting ecocity ideas through environmentalist, preservationist, or civic organizations more their style.

If you are an owner, developer, architect, or planner you can be alert to the mixed-use, high-density ideas and build housing where it coordinates with jobs, providing support for creek restoration, building a minimum of parking spaces for cars and a maximum of facilities for bicyclists and pedestrians. The possibilities are infinite.

There are other ecologically important features of downtowns besides the height of buildings, population densities, and diversity of uses. Fortunately, a concentration of people also means a concentration of capital and real opportunity to invest imaginatively on their behalf in the economy and culture of the downtown. The following are some of the major features contributing to an ecocity downtown.

- *Pedestrian malls, transit malls* (buses or street cars but no automobiles), and *car-free zones* (whole areas, potentially many blocks on a side, in which the private automobile is prohibited). These features create

---

quiet areas promoting convivial connections between people and, compared to auto-dominated streets, providing clean air, greater safety, and conservation of energy. In addition, malls are often favorable environments for business.

- *City art in public places*, especially of the sort that celebrates our place in the bioregion and on the Earth, from sculptures, murals, fountains, creek embankments, and elements of restored shorelines, to beautiful manhole covers—Seattle, with its 1% fee on new development that goes into public art, has many such manhole covers celebrating native American art of the area and including bas relief maps of the downtown.

- *Public amenities* like all-weather awnings and arcades, comfortable benches, shady and sunny areas, and good transit information, such as that provided by computerized transit kiosks in Portland, Oregon.

- *No-car condos and single room housing* (residence hotels and boarding houses.) Single room housing is one of the most affordable ways to live in or near downtowns, where automobile dependence is at a minimum. Many low-income people, students, and singles currently utilize this economical and ecological option. The no-car condo idea is similar but not presently available. Residents of a no-car condo (or apartment) would not be allowed to harbor an automobile, even in a garage somewhere else; for this they should pay lower mortgages or rents since construction and city service costs are lowered if parking and cars are not accommodated. Thus the cost of the condo units would be less than usual and the city would have reasons to lower taxes on the property: those living there would require less services for traffic control, road repair, pollution abatement measures, runoff water treatment, repair and replacement of smog-damaged building materials and clothing, etc. Those living there shouldn't have to subsidize the car drivers. Wealthier people unwilling to give up their cars could still go elsewhere for housing—they always have the best opportunities anyway so they are being denied nothing. In the meantime, the lower-income people would not have the wealthier car-owners competing and driving prices up. The city, as well as lowering taxes on no-car condos, would pass laws to enforce the car prohibition in these buildings.

- *Parking freeze followed by parking reductions.* Few provisions of the present city encourage cars, and thus encourage energy waste, heavier traffic and air pollution, as effectively as "convenient, ample parking." Permit parking that allows residents and special applicants to park in a neighborhood while limiting parking time for others is one good step. High parking costs and expensive parking tickets help, but the positive approach of built-in diversity and good public transportation is better. Minimize parking around malls; add nearby housing instead, thus providing patrons for the businesses on the malls and in the car-free zones.

ACCESS BY PROXIMITY, NOT TRANSPORTATION

Instead of thinking of *going* places, think in terms of *being* places. That is, think in terms of establishing desirable places close to one another. Transportation is what you have to do to get to places inconveniently located: the less the better. For an occasional adventure, transportation is great and the world needs people not only going to foreign places but learning about them in depth and with sympathy. However, when it comes to travel to keep a vital urban lifestyle together, the less that is necessary the healthier your life and your environment. If diversity is designed into the city, commuting is minimized and other local travel can be reserved for special occasions. Cities that are easily navigated without the car—even difficult to manage in a car (Manhattan, downtown San Francisco)—contribute toward increasing train and bus use *between* cities too, since once you get to your destination you can actually get around without bringing or renting a car.

- *There is a hierarchy of ecologically healthier surface transportation modes.* Cars are worst, trains, buses and ferries better, bicycles better yet, and foot travel best. The most serious efforts, then, should be made to help pedestrians, considerable effort made for bicyclists, significant support should be provided public transportation, and strong disincentives should be applied to automobiles.
- *The principle of diversity should moderate the transportation hierarchy.* In other words, many modes should be available, with the greatest emphasis on the pedestrian and the least on the automobile. Car-free zones, pedestrian malls, and transit malls are crucial, with as little adjacent parking as possible. But some cars—for instance, taxis, certain delivery vehicles, and rental cars for getting into rural areas not served by public transportation—could fit into an ecocity context.

A new idea called Slow Streets is being experimented with in

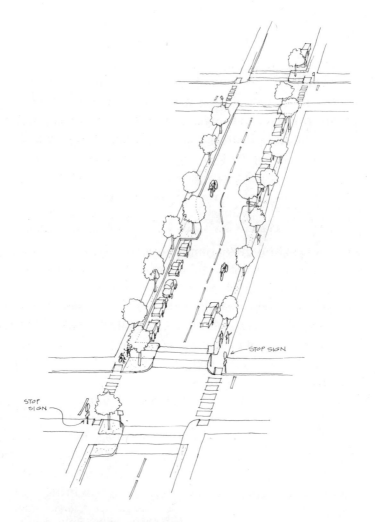

STOP SIGN

STOP
SIGN

SLOW STREET CONCEPT
One of many schemes for slowing traffic.

Berkeley, California. The speed on the route is reduced to a steady non-sweaty bicycle commute speed—approximately 15 miles per hour. Certain design features can be added to help reduce speed: more trees, narrowed curbs at the intersections called "chokers," speed humps (broad bumps in the pavement irritating to car drivers but hardly noticeable to cyclists), and other features. Stop signs should point in the *other* direction, thus aiding in the steady (if reduced-speed) flow of traffic on the Slow Street. Not only bicycles but small, slow vehicles like the electric golf cart-sized vehicle would be encouraged by the Slow Street.

"Woonerf" is the Dutch name for a street that has essentially become a place instead of a route. In hundreds of Dutch and dozens of German cities, selected residential and mixed-use streets have been redesignated for an even greater speed reduction and turned into areas where cars may enter and park, but where the feeling is more like a floor than a street, and where pedestians move among benches, trees, playground equipment, gardens, and sculptures. In fact, on a woonerf the speed limit is so slow that to pass a pedestrian is illegal!

In downtowns and neighborhood centers, bridges between buildings can link public areas above ground level such as rooftop cafes and shops, rooftop gardens, greenhouses, and sports areas. Arcades, awnings, and covered streets make businesses and residences in higher density areas mutually accessible in the worst of weather for foot or bike. Covered bus benches and sheltered train stations are important.

On the anti-negative side, cars should not be given the best shore front, mountain gaps, and other such vistas at the expense of the places where people actually live and work. Freeways should be below ground

A GOOD PLACE FOR FREEWAYS

PRINCIPLES OF ECOCITY BUILDING　　　　　　　　　　　　　35

levels, as they are in many urban areas already, not blocking views. They can even be underground with development on top, as in Freeway Park in Seattle where a beautiful sculptured waterfall and garden park span the traffic. Eventually, freeways could be reduced in size and eliminated, replaced by smaller roads and streets for shorter connections and replaced by rail for longer distance connections. Bridge tolls should be increased for cars to support the other modes.

Bringing about these changes will take time because of the entrenchment of the automobile, its hidden subsidies, and society's associated habits. The faster the change occurs, though, the more we will save of nature and resources for our children. There are two basic approaches to bring about these changes, the personal approach and the organized approach.

In addition to trying to arrange work and home close together, the individual can walk, bike, or take transit, and de-emphasize or give up the automobile (and spend on something else with the $3,500 the American Automobile Association says the average American car owner puts into the car each year). Vote with your money by paying for public transportation. Use the ballot too. And rent cars or share them with others when auto use is unavoidable—and it often will be until cities can be changed into ecocities.

The organizational approach includes design, planning, and political advocacy. Cities have planning and transportation commissions, energy subcommittees, and city councils that must be petitioned. To succeed here, public education and organizational work are necessary. The individual can join or create a group for ecocity purposes, from promoting bicycle lockers at work to rearranging the whole city's zoning for "access by proximity." When useful, groups can join together in coalitions. Neighborhood and environmental groups have a common interest in Slow Streets and woonerfen (plural of woonerf), anti-freeway activists and certain business people could get together to support a development over a freeway—and the city could tax the newly created "land" which was taken off the tax rolls when the state put the freeway in.

A special comment should be made on behalf of protecting railroad right of ways: they should *never* be built upon since they give us the option to rebuild energy-efficient rail transportation—or make great bicycle routes since their grades are gradual and they generally connect concentrations of people (the railroads came along before cars scattered people over vastly larger areas).

Convincing people to rearrange transportation systems is typical of any political activity: new ideas will have to be introduced to the powers that be—and championed until a project is built, a law is passed, a sympathetic candidate elected.

small standard size car covers this much space.

URBAN VEHICLES OF THE FUTURE. Top left: a "cherry picker," in this case picking apples. These could be controlled and driven from the lift bucket, doing jobs from harvesting and repairing aqueducts and monuments to cleaning greenhouses, replacing street lamps and fixing electric lines. Top right: a high speed three-wheeled cycle with clear wind fairing and basket behind the cyclist—for faster streets. Bottom right: small electric cart, dashed line representing optional all-weather dome. Bottom left: double deck bus partially open for the sheer pleasure of riding through a city of fresh air, beautiful gardens, glistening buildings, and greenhouses.

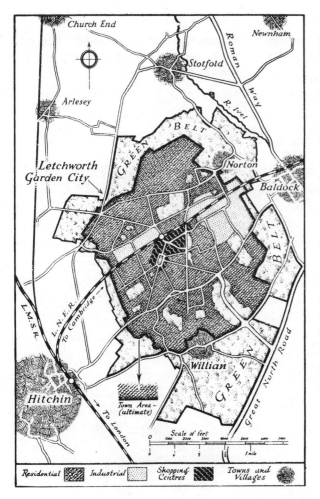

Letchworth, England was designed by Ebenezer Howard and built in 1903 as a "Garden City," a small relatively self-sufficient city surrounded by a "greenbelt" to minimize sprawl and create for its citizens a balance between city and nature. Close to a century later, more than 90% of its 20,000 citizens live and work in the town. Cultural life is as lively as it gets in towns this size, according to many observers, its industries do well, its subsidies from the national government are far lower than average in England, and its public health indicators—infant mortality, longetivity, etc.—are second to only one other town in all of England: Welwyn, Howard's other Garden City, built in 1919.

NEW TOWNS

There are two ways to go about building ecocities: changing existing towns or building new ones.

The best sites for cities, from the perspectives of both human commerce and natural resources, already have cities. But there is still considerable open space where present technologies and timeless agricultural practices could establish new towns and special circumstances keep them viable. College towns, research centers, retirement communities, supply depots like logging towns or fishing villages, are less diverse than larger cities but can serve worthy ends—and could be buit along ecocity guidelines. Furthermore, they could use ecocity insights to do it right the first time. Instead of correcting mistakes by creek restoration and withdrawal from sprawl, these cities could leave the creeks open in the first place and build compactly with diversity integrated at every stage.

The new towns of Ebenezer Howard in England, like Letchworth Garden City and ones in America like Reston, Virginia, were a start. Paolo Soleri's Arcosanti, Arizona, is perhaps the most ambitious and inspired—certainly the most radical—step toward land and energy conservation, compactness and social vitality and diversity yet attempted. Arcosanti aspires to be small town—about 6,000 people—that would amount to an "urban laboratory" in the high desert of Arizona, a laboratory dedicated to testing certain elements of Soleri's ecocity design concept which he calls arcology, a term synthesizing architecture and ecology. I say "certain elements of" because such a small town hardly gives full test to an urban design concept, as Soleri himself acknowledges. But even if a (relatively) small start, the basic idea there is to build the entire community in a single interlinked structure, a town like a large building of many connected wings rising over but not covering or suffocating the natural landscape.

Cerro Gordo is a more modest small-town effort planned to eventually house 2,500 residents near Cottage Grove, Oregon. Since its inception the project has publicized the concept that families should live in communities that consciously limit their impact on the ecosphere. Its members were part of the "back to the land" movement of the early seventies . . . and many members are still hanging on as new people join in. Cerro Gordo struggled for ten years to get its primarily agricultural, forestry, and small manufacturing community plan accepted by county officials. In 1985 they finally succeeded. A small amount of existing construction, say the community organizers, will soon be augmented with enough new building to create a real village, and one aspiring to ecological health and stability. While waiting for the plan to be accepted, some of the potential Cerro Gordo community members moved to neighboring Cottage Grove and set up several businesses (one of them builds light-weight bicycle trailers which could also be eventually used on their car-less village streets). Soon these businesses will move into their new mixed-use community of clustered buildings. Cars will have to park outside the village and, if all goes well, the community of families will grow slowly into a stable and sustainable village consciously limiting its ecological impact, growing salable food and timber, and taking care to keep its small lake

ARCOSANTI, ARIZONA, 1986

healthy and clean.

Early experiments give us some solid experience to learn from; we need new prototypes and they should get society's support since they are genuine pioneering projects bringing us crucial information. As Lewis Mumford said of Letchworth, the cost of building the whole city as an experiment turned out to be financially cheaper than paying for the usual government studies to prove one thing or another about how it might work out—and the lessons learned from actual cities built and functioning are from experience, not speculation. Meantime, the people are served directly, that the studies would supposedly serve indirectly—if ever anything were actually built, and if in fact the studies were not interpreted in the usual way to mean that nothing like that *could* be built. But thanks to people like Ebenezer Howard, there is no question that the new town approach can work.

How to build from scratch? First, the vision needs to be clear. Then several things have to come about roughly together. A developer or group of people need to plan the community while forming a corporation for this purpose and for locating considerable investment capital. Meantime it has to be clear that people would want to live there and be able to support themselves with remunerative work: jobs need to be planned in. Also, the local county will have to be convinced that the new town would be an asset and not just another loss of often much-loved open space.

If all these things are coming along well, physical planning can proceed realistically, and pretty much according to the principles laid out here for transforming existing towns. That is, with planned-in diversity, maximum care for preserving and celebrating nature in this special place, with relative compactness and minimal acquiesce to automobiles, maximum care to conserve energy and transform wastes to new resources.

THE LAW

If American building codes, city ordinances and zoning—even solar access and personal liability laws—were applied retroactively to the wonderful old cities of Europe, the Second World War would look friendly in comparison: it would *all* have to go. Too many people live in spaces too small and odd-shaped served by too little electricity— not enough safety features: too few walls around canals, often no banisters on steps which are usually too steep or narrow, too few giant signs for speeding cars, wide roads, bright street lights at night. The narrow streets of the old city centers would run afoul of solar access regulations. Many trees, especially fruit and nut trees, would have to be eliminated. Their crime: producing nutritious food that can fall with a squish into the public domain.

Some laws are in the way of ecocities, some help. In any case, there needs to be major changes in the law, in the United States from the Constitution down. Remember, *any* old law can be changed or nullified and *any* new law can be legislated and upheld in court if there is enough support. (One hopes the goodness of the law and the support for it coincide. . . .)

Local hiring and other "proximity policies" are considered unconstitutional, though some cities get away with quietly promoting "hire local" campaigns. In theory, proximity policies discriminate against long-distance commuters. And yet the effect of such frequent and far-flung travel is catastrophic long-term destruction of environment, both natural and urban, and discriminates against everyone, present and future. Nobody could be faulted for not giving a job, loan, or rental space in his or her office or house to someone known to be inconsiderate to others or actively dangerous. And who could be more dangerous than the Automobile Driver, who every year mows down more than 45,000 people in the United States in accidents while maiming several hundred thousand more, and kills several thousand others by respiratory and heart disease? Laws should apply this awareness to city development by establishing a wide range of proximity policies. Loans, jobs, and housing should be available preferentially to those who are moving to or live near activity centers and downtowns.

National laws subsidizing construction need to be changed. For

---

instance, the federal government presently pays 90% for highway construction costs, the state puts up 10%. The feds pay 80% to cities and regional agencies for transit; the local contribution: 20%. That means for every dollar put up locally, the federal government puts $9.00 into subsidizing the car and $4.00 into transit. This and many other national laws which subsidize ecologically unhealthy arrangements need to be changed for everybody's eventual benefit, from our progeny and the endangered species to the Automobile Club and highway-lobby members who work so hard and effectively for Auto Sprawl Syndrome (and their legislated financial privileges). In some larger sense, we all need clean air, energy conservation, ample farm land, transportation safety. . . .

One of the main reasons for shifting subsidies is to encourage people to live closer to the centers since in these locations they have the healthiest impact on living nature, resources and the city itself. Those presently living at a distance are subsidized: by cheap finite fossil fuels, inexpensive land, banking practices that make loans available to suburbs and not lower-income urban areas, by the subsidization of water, sewage, and garbage services, and by a disproportionate share of city and state street and highway maintenance. The point of ecocity zoning, proximity laws and subsidies is to reward those that have positive or minimum effect on living systems, rather than those who stress them. Regulation and subsidy are part and parcel of all systems of governance, whether on the national or local scale, regardless of rhetoric about freeing people from government. They should be a means of accomplishing common goals, performing the public benefit. Ecocity subsidies, and zoning (which will be described later) rearranges things for the public health in a new context: the long-term health of the bioregion, the human species and the planet itself.

State laws establishing uniform standards for street design and street signs need to be loosened to allow cities to come up with their own unique solutions. Because of present uniform street signing laws in California, it is not legal to enforce a 15 mile per hour speed limit on a Slow Street. Laws should be written to define Slow Streets and woonerfen and allow posting of appropriate signs. The freer cities are to come up with their own solutions, the more each will take on characteristics that reflect its own special character, that fit its own bioregion, history, and attitudes.

Fruit and nut trees are illegal along the streets of most cities. This is because some owners fail to harvest or clean up under their fruit trees, thus creating an aesthetic offense in other people's eyes and a liability if someone were to step on a fruit and slip. Both objections are legitimate but could be reduced in two ways. First, establish a legal procedure for taking responsibility for the trees: either the city hires a roving orchard-farmer (city employees presently trim ornamental street trees in any case), or the landowner who wants the trees accepts responsibility for upkeep, and for liability and penalty. In this same spirit, the food-tree lover could strategically plant trees with soft fruit (plums, peaches, and some pears) where they do not overhang sidewalks, while reserving nuts and harder fruit (apples and lemons) for the more public locations. Second—and this is a matter of degree—people should take responsibility for themselves. To slip and fall on a sidewalk because of a fruit should not yield a gigantic settlement for the unalert person—a small settlement based on shared responsibility would make sense. Perhaps people who can't trust their own awareness should insure themselves; laws certainly should encourage transfer of a good deal of responsibility back to the individual. The many lawyers who sit in legislatures don't tend to like such laws, which reduce their money-making opportunities, but would nonetheless not only help establish urban orchards but encourage many other elements of ecocities.

THE ECOCITY ADVENTURE

From the perspective of the nineteen fifties, the future looked like an exciting place to be. Cars controlled by electric eyes would be guided across beautiful open countryside while driver and passenger would sit facing one another playing cards. No crowds, no smog on the smooth superhighway—idylic farmlands and scenic America unmarred in that vision by billboards, high-tension lines, crumpled litter and endless waves of repetitive housing. Labor-saving robots would cook and serve the food, vacuum the carpet, cut the lawn. Peace would be guaranteed; technology would simply deliver us better living through chemistry. Space-travel would be a wonderful adventure and automobiles sprouted rocket tailfins in anticipation.

In the sixties the image of the future became painfully vague: the Age of Aquarius had all the clarity, discipline, and commitment of a wishful daydream. A good deal was done for the here and now, but not much to build a healthy, secure, exciting future.

By the seventies and eighties, having lost a war against a small nation, having gone to the Moon with a stiff American flag and been briefly excited, then after a few repetitions, being somewhat bored by it all, having watched technology's tarnishing pollution and terrifying nuclear arms race make an absurdity of "Progress," Americans began to long for not a future but a past they imagined to be a *relief* from the future. Add this to the ecologist's predictions of massive biospherical damage and energy experts' warnings of impending shortages and it is no wonder so many people are now far from upbeat about conjuring a better future. Having learned what we have over the past three decades, hopeful visions would look naive in the extreme, right?

Wrong! The vision of ecologically healthy technologies, lifestyles,

VISIONS—VIOLENCE VS. CREATIVITY: Above: Star Wars, from childhood video games to American international policy—current mainstream visions of the future. Irrelevant or prophetic? If irrelevant, so what? If prophetic, a sad commentary on humanity's maturity, compassion, creativity . . . and prospects.

Right: Built environments can be exciting and imaginative, bringing nature up to the urban edge. Being comfortable and secure is important part of the time, but we may learn, with deeper self-knowledge, that a certain edge of creative tension, discomfort, insecurity, healthy stress, and exercise is necessary to most people's sense of being a lively participant in life, of being fully alive and at home. Construction is a relatively dangerous occupation—which is one of its virtues: it is a far better way to give of one's self, to use one's strength and skill, to take risks, than to pursue visions of worth through conflict.

Building and living in exciting, challenging, beautiful cities is a better game than war. And, whereas war lies about its essence—otherwise it would find no recruits—building ecocities is an honest confrontation with problems of our times.

and towns and cities is not an impossible dream but an attainable one that jibes with both necessity and human imagination, with taking responsibility for our actions upon the world and with granting to ourselves exciting possibilities for our own fuller development. It's realistic and visionary simultaneously. There are other important aspects to the ecocity adventure.

When Rambo, war toys (euphemistically called "action toys" in the eighties), and simplistic television violence suggest something of a future in which we become real men and real heroines again, we are being had. Creativity, not destruction, will be the adventure of the future, in sync with nature and not against it. Either that or we can blame only ourselves when our children curse us for despoiling their world. Said William James, "What we now need to discover in the social realm is the moral equivalent of war; something heroic that will speak to man as universally as war does, and yet will be as compatible with their spiritual selves as war has proved to be incompatible." Many people seem to need the experience of risk, of danger, of being part of something larger than the self, and of going to exotic, exciting places. So *build* them! (The opposite of climbing the mountain because it is there is building because it isn't.)

The physical acts of creativity go a long way toward delivering adventure to its explorers. Challenge, mastery of self and one's own work, and results that make the creative person part of something larger than the self are all aspects of building a new kind of city. Construction is sometimes dangerous, often exhilirating, and useful work. The aesthetic possibilities are extremely rich when nature and living ecosystems are brought into the new building projects. Seeking relevance to a healthy future by way of energy conservation, recycling, and so on is a healthier and more understanding way to secure a worthwhile life for our children than preparing to extinguish "enemies" we spend virtually no time trying to understand.

Some people have recently been carrying out an "architecture of peace:" buildings, monuments, and designed landscapes providing peaceful settings or symbolizing the concerns of peace.

Ecocities represent a *functional* architecture of peace—in two important ways: first, humanity is not only at war with itself but also with nature. Ecocities go a long way to actually ending that destructive, war-like relationship with nature—a big step and a good model. Second, if we can come up with a healthy, realizable vision of the future and our roles and work in it, we will begin to define what it is we need to build to bring it about. We begin to define jobs. Economic conversion from a war economy to a peace economy can only occur if we find new work for millions of people. To make conversion a reality we will have to know what it is we actually *need* to make and build, what sort of services to provide. Ecocities go a long way toward clarifying that, thereby making a conversion much more likely.

Perhaps most important, as those who have gone to Arcosanti to help, who have struggled for Cerro Gordo in Oregon, or worked with Urban Ecology in Berkeley can attest, there is room for everybody in the ecocity effort. It is not vicarious but participatory, not to be dictated, but to be created in a million ways simultaneously from the grassroots to the highest levels of planning and back down again, with a role for each of us. Ecocity building is an accessible adventure and one of the most promising ones imaginable. And, we will assuredly embark upon this adventure as soon as we get serious about assuring a healthy future.

NOTES ON STRATEGY

In the course of this book, suggestions are made for implementing eco-city ideas. Anyone who actually sets out to help build ecocities can benefit by keeping several things about strategy in mind.

Appeal to people's interests, all kinds, both selfish and generous. In ecocity buiding it is also appropriate to appeal to interests in the deep future and the whole Earth. We should never assume people don't care about these things, fashionable though cynicism and selfishness may be in the eighties. Many people simply haven't had sufficient positive exposure to such ideas. That's our job. *And* some people are mostly selfish—no point in being naive about that. Try to convince them only if it looks possible and worthwhile. Save energy for others more sympathetic. Even some pretty nasty people change, but usually at their own pace and after a good many others change first; so approaching others will affect the unsympathetic more than approaching them directly. Only serious commitment of time and money will build ecologically healthy cities. "Sacrifices" can be investments—and a lot of fun. Assume you're going to have to pay a significant sum to make major changes in your yard or your house. Tithe yourself or tax your car a penny a mile for a group that's working for ecocities. Vote for bond issues, taxes, assessment districts, and candidates who realize serious money is needed for change. Volunteer for organizations. Go to public hearings occasionally: they are an opportunity to exercise your sacred duty—I'm serious—to speak out for a better future; citizen participation makes a very big difference.

In issues of local development, *only* develop *if* it's good development. Promote considerable development and take responsibility in your community for much needed housing and jobs, but only if they are in the right places and include major investments in ecocity features. People need places to live and work and shouldn't be forced into sprawl due to exclusionary city and neighborhood policies and attitudes. If developers don't like the deal, don't let them build. If they insist on inappropriate development, let them try to mess up some other place. If other places won't let them, they will eventually build ecocities—and be well appreciated for their work. Providing for people at a time of growing population and displaced populations is a responsibility of the city, and so is doing it in a healthy manner.

Some neighborhood residents and businesses will feel the pinch of change toward ecocities. But if they receive generous compensation and if the policies are applied to the whole city, it will be acknowledged as fair and receive much wider support than a piecemeal neighborhood by neighborhood approach with little forethought about compensation. Neighborhoods and businesses are generally conservative—and with many good reasons. Yet we need change. A strategy that works with and for the whole city has the best chance of success.

Finally, remember that anything is possible if enough people are with you; everything is impossible if enough are against you. Education of self and others, and with real sensitivity, is of the highest importance. It all starts—or fails to start—with each of us. As Margaret Mead said. "Never doubt that a small group of thoughtful, committed citizens can change the world: indeed, it's the only thing that ever has."

Now to develop some examples, let's take a look at possibilities for Berkeley, California. As your read Part II, keep your own town in mind, and if you do, you will discover more and more special, unique things about your city, solutions to its own problems and contributions it can make to other towns. The better we understand the basic ecocity principles, the richer and livelier our local society, biology and agriculture will become. In rewriting Part II for your own city, consult liberally with your children, who will inherit the city. Their ideas will sometimes be brilliant and sometimes sound crazy—but remember nothing can be as crazy as the hair-trigger nuclear nightmare we've already bestowed upon them, and remember the outlandishly beautiful dreams they come up with could all be possible if our own dreams of dominance of nature and each other were toned down and resources were freed for healthy, creative works. Together, our children and we can take the big step of imagining a better world with better cities. Write it all down, and if you take care to consider nature, it will amount to your own local Part II of this book.

Then . . . good luck in building your ecocity.

Part 2

...BERKELEY

BERKELEY BEACH AND MARSH
BEFORE ARRIVAL OF EUROPEANS

Beach on the left, marsh in the middle with the brush-covered promentory called El Cerrito, end of beach, and Albany Hill surmounted on the right by a typical summer cloud of fog. In the words of an early explorer, this was "a land of inexpressible fertility."

THE NATURAL ENDOWMENT

Berkeley is situated on the eastern shoreline of the San Francisco Bay directly opposite and downwind from the Golden Gate. Out through the gate, the Pacific Ocean stretches eight thousand miles to the Orient. In through the gate tendrils of summer fog often reach across the bay from the sea to cool and moisten Berkeley, while just north and south other East Bay cities may be toasting in the sunshine under clear blue skies. It's a variation on the regional coastal theme called a Mediterranean climate: dry in the hot season, moderately rainy in the cool season; almost never freezes.

Before the arrival of the Europeans, the Bay Area was one of the richest ecological zones on Earth. The stately Sacramento River flowed into the Bay from the north, snaking through a grand marsh many times larger than the Bay itself, pushing out against the ocean tides, mixing with and freshening the waters in the Bay, bringing silt and nutrients from the mountain slopes of the Coastal Range and the Sierra Nevada. The South Bay was relatively still, with high evaporation and high salt content. Dozens of year-round and some seasonal creeks tumbled off the hills into the bay terminating in muddy, fresh and salt water marshes or passing through clean sandy beaches. It was a wonderfully rich and diverse undergirding for an even more complex texture of living ecosystems and creatures of land, air, and sea.

The area that is now Berkeley had nine creeks, the larger ones home to steelhead trout, salmon, and several smaller species of fish. In the Bay there were clams, mussels, oysters, crabs, shrimp, skates, rays, sharks, sardines, rockfish, and the prehistoric sturgeon, looking like a cross between a shark, catfish and crocodile, some over a thousand pounds and more than ten feet long, gliding along the bottoms.

Occasionally a whale would wash up on the beach among otters and seals to the pleasure of clans of wandering grizzleybears and wolves.

Above waterline, a low, undulating grassland commenced behind the beaches, reeds, and marshes and spread east to the hills in several wide stripes divided by the creeks and their greener bushes and trees. Occasional oaks dotted the rolling hills covered with shoulder-high perennial bunch grass; bay laurel and magnificent redwoods 200 feet tall marched up the short canyons in the hills, creating still, cool, nearly silent environments. Like cathedrals, these trees created awe-inspiring interiors with tall collumns reaching to a canopy, and through reddish branches and green foliage, the blue and white sky, made lace work windows casting beams of light into the darkened cavern. Fringing these small forests of giants, scattered madrone trees with their luminous yellow-green leaves, red-orange berries, and smooth salmon-to-rust-colored skin with large chartreuse patches created worlds inside that seemed to glow like sources of their own warm light, each madrone a dome-shaped home to countless buzzing, noisy insects. Between the stripes of grassy undulations and marshes near the waterfront, just a few feet under the surface, or actually covering it, water was everywhere seeping and trickling into the Bay. Creeks passing through these areas would flood or drain them depending on time of year. On the salt fringes grew pickleweed, tule reed, and cord-grass—one of the richest, most biologically productive environments on Earth.

The animals visiting these wet lands and watercourses, wandering these savannahs singly or in herds of up to many hundreds, included rabbits, foxes, coyotes, mountain lions, deer, elk, antelope, and bear. Overhead, migrating birds by the millions touched down in the Bay Area, swirling in clouds that sometimes blotted out large patches of sky on Berkeley's bay shore. Geese, ducks, cormorants, snipe, gulls, pelicans, cranes, and herons, around the water; grouse, quail, jays on or over the land; and high above, the dizzying wheeling of vultures, ravens, hawks, eagles and, largest of all, the majestic condors with their ten foot wingspan. From inches above still water and grassy lands, to so high they could barely be seen, swallows and other fly catchers enjoyed dinner at a hundred miles an hour rocketing through the sky in straight lines, wide arcs or yanking off in right angle turns at 5 Gs.

In those days before the Europeans arrived, Berkeley and its immediate surroundings were a land of "inexpressible fertility," in the words of an early explorer. The local Ohlone Indian "tribelet," the Huchiun, had minor effect on all this richness, sharing it peacefully with other small Indian villages in the area, despite a bewildering variety of mutually unintelligible languages.

The Europeans were another story. Not only could they not get along with other human beings, first enslaving, then almost extinguishing the Indians, they also couldn't suffer the omnipresence of all those all-too-edible varmints.

Today, most aquatic species are drastically reduced through over fishing and water contamination. Spawning grounds in the creeks are cut off from the ocean by miles of closed pipe and box culverts—most of the creeks for almost all of their reach in Berkeley have become "storm drains." A large fraction of the Sacramento's fresh water is now diverted to farmers in California's Central Valley and south to the lawns, pools, houses, and car washes of the Los Angeles megalopolis. Sixty percent of the water that used to flow into the Bay is now diverted—which compounds the pollution problem: it used to take the fresh river water and shifting tides 2.4 months to thoroughly recycle the Bay water; now it takes 13.3 months. The salinity of the Bay has also been altered by the reduced flow of fresh water, and now, one third of the Bay has been filled and *ninety-five percent* of the marshes and nurseries for small fish have been covered with housing, dumps, farms, freeways, military fields, San Francisco high rise buildings, airports. . . .

In Berkeley, the freeway, U.S. 880, was built on the beach areas of the south part of Berkeley and on the marshes of the northern shoreline, destroying at one blow both the best areas for waterfront recreation and the most important ecological resource in the area.

The creeks now unceremoniously pop out of concrete tubes, carrying their burden of oil, rubber dust, powdered asbestos brake lining, smog soot, dog feces hosed off lawns and into the gutters, and small amounts of exotic chemicals from the University of California's labs.

From this sad stretch of rubble dumps, muddy tires, and rumbling freeway traffic called a shoreline, the city of Berkeley now spreads as a relatively uniform one- to two-story settlement into the Berkeley Hills. Population densities generally rise toward the center of town and the University campus, which adjoins downtown near the foot of the hills. Sparsely-used University land spreads from there up into the hills, a strip heading east from downtown with a campus of 29,000 students and 4,500 staff and faculty at the west end of the property, a few scattered large buildings on the hills to the east. Steep, slippery slopes (high-clay-content soil) and the active Hayward Fault line have been virtually ignored: north and south of the University land, some of the most expensive houses in town are built on the hills, and a small nuclear research reactor straddles the fault. Some home owners are constantly struggling to keep their houses from slithering down the hill. No major earthquakes have occured since the reactor was built.

With the exception of a few rare stretches, creeks are everywhere underground, often under buildings. Needless to say, very little remains of the original deer, rabbits, raccoons, wildcats, snakes, lizards, salamanders, and native birds that still reside here—but they are a starting point for rebuilding a vital animal population. Someday maybe eagles, long absent sea birds, and foxes will return and, if we dare dream a little, sprawl will contract to the point that great areas of land are opened up again and antelope and condors will grace our lives as they did the lives of those who came before us. The authors of Berkeley's Master Plan identify the contemporary city as "built up" and put forward the notion that there is little room for more development; they of course don't ever consider the possibility of the withdrawal of development where it exists, for natural, agricultural, or any other uses. This situation of ecological poverty and lack of imagination doesn't have to continue. In fact it's heartening to consider that nothing does continue very long in human or ecological affairs. We can do better— and we will if we decide to.

Now we'll look at the city, one aspect of it at a time, creeks, neighborhoods, transportation, downtown. . . . And when we have some sense of all those details we'll weave them all together in an overall pattern for reshaping Berkeley in a forty to one-hundred-and fifty year strategy.

CREEKS

Creeks are blood vessels for the living tissue of the earth, bringing water and nourishment to all varieties of plants and animals, whether they live in the water, on the banks, or come there to drink and find food. Creeks and other waterways are among the richest ecological zones and greatest sources of pleasure for people of all ages, but especially children. In Berkeley, creeks are mostly buried—but far from forgotten.

Several organizations have cooperated in attempts to help the Berkeley creeks. One short section was uncovered in 1984 on the old Santa Fe Railroad right-of-way (which the company donated to the City). Other parts of the same land became open lawns and play area (now called Strawberry Creek Park). There is a local Urban Creeks Council which anyone can join. Several very sympathetic individuals are members of the City's Parks and Recreation Commission. The parts of the creeks that are open are fairly clean of debris and garbage— which is politically advantageous for creek lovers since litter is often used as rationale for covering creeks. And there is now a "creeks preservation ordinance" which allows covering of creeks only after a public hearing, if then. In other words, Berkeley is off to a good start in respect to creek restoration.

Fredric Law Ulmstead, designer of New York's Central Park, visited Berkeley in the 1860s and proclaimed the creeks to be among the town's most important assets. This famous and historically important landscape designer proposed designs that would keep the creeks open; this precedent can be used to promote creek restoration at any time, now and in the future. Fred Cody, owner of one of Berkeley's best bookstores, was a legendary good guy in Berkeley's recent past, a contributor to many causes, and a source of positive spirit and true imagination.

Two years before he died of cancer in 1985 he suggested a restoration strategy that would begin by focusing on one creek from spring to Bay: Strawberry Creek, Berkeley's largest and best known.

Cody pointed out that along almost all of its run through campus and up into the hills, the creek is open. In two additional short stretches, at Strawberry Creek Park and just upstream for two blocks, it is also open. The creek runs close to the surface under a park behind City Hall, and under parking lots and playing fields at two schools; much of the rest of its course is under and around low-density housing. It is, in other words, an almost ideal creek around which to build a restoration project. In fact, even without such an overall strategy, one year after Cody's death, the Downtown Planning Group is suggesting that, where the creek passes under the pavement of the highest density part of Berkeley, a street or an alley could be converted to a pedestrian area and the creek exposed to the sun and air.

Next steps in the plan might follow like this: The downtown stretch could be opened up with money from city funds and a downtown assessment district, now under consideration by Berkeley's downtown business community could be established. (An assessment district is an alliance in which business people, or any other people owning property in an area, pool their money for community projects that benefit themselves and the part of town where they do business or own property.)

The city already owns the old West Campus facilities for Berkeley High School; these were under-utilized in 1986 and closed as far as high school classes go. The creek runs under a playing field there, recently converted to a parking lot, and could be opened with little expense.

A special new strategy is needed for areas where the creek passes under residential lots. Here the city should attempt to gain first right of refusal on any house that comes up for sale. Money from taxes, bonds, raised by creek support organizations, or channelled from the State for creek improvements, or any combination of these could be assembled in a fund for buying houses over or near creeks. The city could even make offers on houses at or above market rates and include money to help occupants move. Combining social equity with ecological values requires that the city should also see that new comparable housing is made available at a rate that exceeds housing losses because of creek restoration and other forms of withdrawal from once and future natural and agricultural land.

As progress is made on the Fred Cody Memorial Strawberry Creek

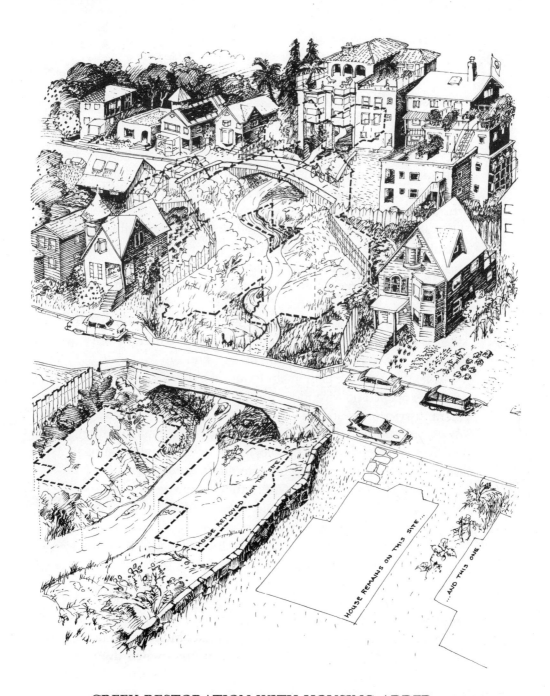

CREEK RESTORATION WITH HOUSING ADDED

Dashed lines represent nine houses removed to open up a creek and provide fifteen apartment units. The apartments are closer to downtown or the neighborhood activity center than the houses in the foreground. One of them, with the Earth flag and trombe wall, is built on top of the old street. There is no access to the courtyard over the arched bridge for cars—bikes and pedestrians only. Foot and bike passageways permit people to go between the apartments and through the center of the block toward the activity center.

Restoration Project (why not a bronze plaque at a special place along the creek?), creeks in other parts of town can benefit from the lessons generated on Strawberry.

A number of private land owners have done beautiful work in planting and landscaping around stretches of Codornices Creek. The city could support such good work by reducing taxes for these owners and thus encourage such people to stay on as stewards of the creek.

Ultimately, all the creeks would be opened up again. Salmon and steelhead could return to their spawning grounds. For a short season, fishing poles would appear in downtown Berkeley—an unusual business people's lunch break. Sculptural aqueducts, fountains, and fish ladders could celebrate the creek's progress through town, freshening the air, bringing back dragonflies, songbirds, bats, frogs, turtles, lily pads, watercress, cattails—a vital city within a city, a natural one threading through the one made by people.

BERKELEY WATERFRONT

The view from Berkeley's waterfront across the bay, out the Golden Gate and over the Pacific Ocean is immortalized on the Great Seal of the State of California. Lest that view become as extinct as the California Grizzly Bear on the same seal, care needs to be taken to keep that part of town in something close to the natural condition.

The situation in 1986 is this: the same Santa Fe Land Company that donated its right of way to Berkeley, now wants to build several million square feet of commercial development on the former marsh and present landfill. There is already a busy marina, several restaurants, and a hotel on the bay fill. A proposed compromise development that has a good chance of success would place a half million square feet of hotels and conference rooms on the old marsh. Another proposal features two and three story commercial buildings along the freeway on top of the former marsh. This "North Basin Strip" is cut off from the Oceanview Neighborhood by fourteen lanes of traffic, most of it U.S. I-880 (the freeway), several railroad tracks, and four blocks of industrial development. There is no way this development could make graceful and easy foot or bicycle contact available between the North Basin freeway strip and jobs, homes, services, and community amenities. The distances are too great, the crossing unpleasant in the extreme. The linear arrangement of the proposed development makes it inefficient to serve by bus. The area is, in other words, whether residential or business, isolated and automobile-dependent.

Santa Fe, however, has legal rights to develop the land. They own it, and, even if the city or state decided to claim the area as an important public resource and zone it for open space or exercise eminent domain rights, Santa Fe would have to be compensated. But if the

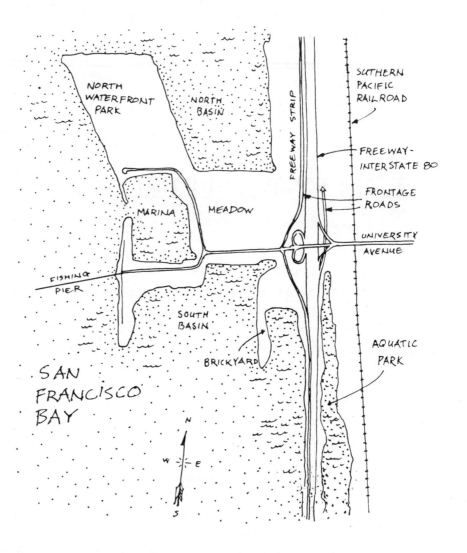

SAN FRANCISCO BAY

Figure 1. PRESENT OUTLINES

Waterfront proposals before the city in 1986 assume these outlines will remain, a strange assumption since they didn't exit at all forty years ago before
the freeway and the dumping. Looking ahead one century, and assuming our
society's technology does not utterly collapse, we might as well look at an
optimal set of changes that makes room for 1.) considerable development
providing housing, workspace, jobs, services, 2.) ecological regeneration along
with optimal water circulation, beach building, creek restoration, and 3.) imaginative, beautiful changes, both in the built environment and restored natural
environment, and 4.) healthy transportation, energy and farming alternatives.

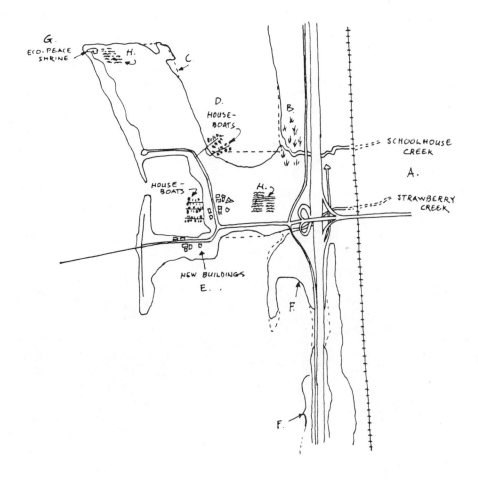

Figure 2. FIVE TO FIFTEEN YEARS

A. Strawberry and Schoolhouse creeks are on their way to being restored, run open and through large, airy tunnels under the roads to the railroad tracks.

B. Dredging out some fill on Schoolhouse Creek's former delta area brings back a few acres of marsh with small stands of cordgrass and new shrimp, crabs, frogs, turtles, birds . . .

C. Dashed lines represent old shoreline, solid lines represent new shoreline created by shifting fill and dredging.

D. A new houseboat community established in the North Basin.

E. New development—buildings by Santa Fe Land Company or other developers beginning to create a real village.

F. Sand is being added here to extend the beach.

G. Eco/Peace Center/Museum: foot, bicycle and disabled vehicle access.

H. Farming

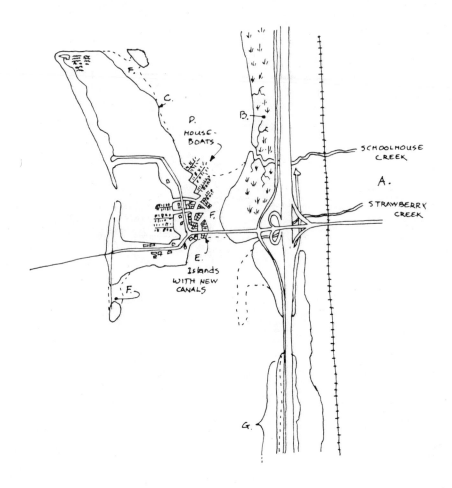

Figure 3. FIFTEEN TO FIFTY YEARS

A. Strawberry Creek is now 100% open, mouth to spring, Schoolhouse Creek 80% open.
B. Dredging has continued on the marsh and now it is quite significant, supporting many re-established species, and together with such restoration projects around the Bay, has increased the fishery noticeably.
C. Shoreline now altered so that the Marina area becomes three islands rather than an artificial peninsula, improving water circulation. Brickyard peninsula is now gone.
D. Houseboat community expands and moves closer to the Marina village.
E. Dredging and filling creates islands and canals—like Venice or Amsterdam—and the population continues to increase.
F. Channels created by dredging.
G. Added sand makes for a wide beach.

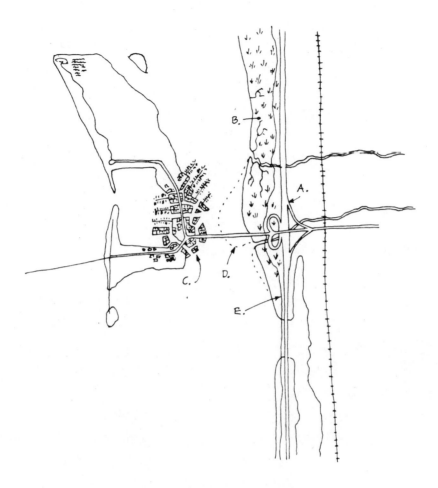

Figure 4. THIRTY TO ONE HUNDRED YEARS

A. As fossil fuels dwindle, railroads prosper and cities are being reconstructed on the basis of diversity at close proximity, the freeway shrinks.

B. The marsh is now quite substantial; enormous numbers of waterfowl and fish are nurtured here.

C. Still more canal dredging and island building.

D. Last dredging of the old "meadow."

E. Frontage road west of freeway is removed, a bicycle path established.

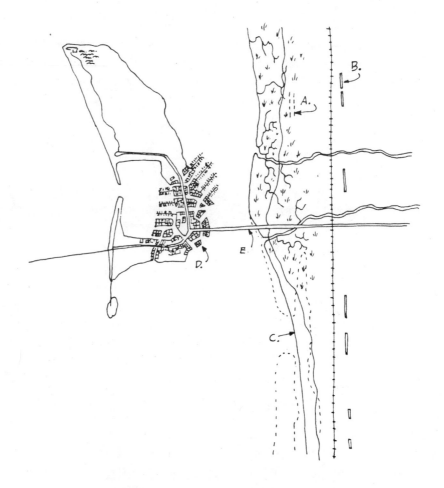

Figure 5. ONE HUNDRED TO ONE HUNDRED FIFTY YEARS
A. Old freeway location.
B. New freeway is only four lanes and is located underground—skylights visible as long dashed lines. Outside city areas, freeway is not covered, but few use it; many more use rail.
C. New shoreline is very close to the original; wide beach all the way south from Strawberry Creek's mouth.
D. Growth virtually stops at the island village. The fishing industry in the Bay now maintains a high, sustainable yield.
E. University Avenue causeway brings streetcars to the North Waterfront Park terminis and to the foot of the pier.

city offered a transfer of development rights to another part of town, tax deferment, and services to Santa Fe as reasonable compensation, why not have the development shifted somewhere else so that the beach and marsh could one day be restored? Development could be relocated to one or more of the main centers: Downtown, Oceanview, or the Adeline/Ashby area, once known as Lorin. The City could offer a transfer of development rights to Santa Fe Land Company and do one of several things or a mix of them: buy up land and run-down or low-density buildings in these centers and offer to trade them for Santa Fe land on the waterfront, and/or offer a package of tax forgiveness (not charging tax on property) until Santa Fe has saved as much money in taxes as the property would have cost, and include in the offering a waiver of building-permit fees and such city services as planning-staff time and real-estate work locating properties for the trade, working out the legalities and language of the trade, and so on. Courts would probably have to decide the value of the waterfront land as the first step. And the process would undoubtedly take considerable time, while the city and various groups of citizens interested in the area could raise money and begin buying properties for the trade.

Transfer of development rights is not a new legal tool, but should be refined and taken much farther than at present. It could become one of the major strategy tools in reshaping cities for purposes of ecological health. If Santa Fe Land Company did not want to accept the Berkeley offer, the offer would have a good chance of standing up in court: a sincere transfer-of-development-rights offer for the public benefit, and recognizing prior ownership rights of the land company.

Other possible locations for development include land immediately adjacent to the existing Marina complex or already owned by the hotel, Marina, or one of the restaurants. Remove some lawns and parking lots, for example. The city owns most of the land there, and, outrageously enough from the ecological point of view, most of it is parking—in spite of good public transit. And so, a land trade with substantial development rights to Santa Fe would be well within the realm of possibility. The Marina already has enough visitors, along with some houseboat dwellers, that neighborhood stores and some jobs could be built into new office and housing on the site. Venice-like canals could be dredged at this location, and buildings constructed at densities comparable to Venice's. If it sounds fanciful (and some have said so) it's useful to remind ourselves that the founders of Venice, Amsterdam, Soochow, and other watercourse cities were technologically far less

BERKELEY'S VENICE VILLAGE: Above: Fog rolls through the Golden Gate obscuring the bridge while Mount Tamalpais rises in the background. Schoolhouse Creek meanders to the beach at low tide; salt water pours into the tributaries at high tide. Various crabs, shellfish, shrimp, snails, otters, and racoons inhabit this zone of nutrient-rich mud and cordgrass. Local birds include sandpipers, blackbirds, gulls, cormorants, ducks, coots, herons, egrets. At the leading edge of the fog is a large sailing ship with new metal sails.

Right: Zooming in on the drawing above we see the mixed-use town with canals and bridges. Trees shelter these buildings from the often-cool winds; windmills utilize the air flow to generate electricity and pump water. The marina is mostly behind the trees, on the foggy side; some of the house-boat community is there, some off-picture to the right. This is a fishing village with hotels, conference center, (small) tourism, crafts and trades, offices, apartments, schools, cafes, bars. Accessed by causeway, bus bike, and ferries; very near the Peace/Ecology Center/Museum.

developed than we: no concrete, steel, earthmovers, gasoline, electricity, computers. If we could catch up to their aesthetics, imagination, foresight, and willpower, our task would be *easy* compared to the job they faced. In fact many new island/canal developments exist: to mention just a few in California: Venice, Thousand Oaks, and in the Bay Area in particular, Foster City, and Belvedere.

The bus service already provided to the Marina would function more efficiently with a larger population adjacent to the existing

facilities. Adding the linear development along the freeway rather than at the Marina, would create the need for a new, inefficient bus route while not adding much to patronage of the existing line: a double loser for transit.

The only hope for reducing the freeway's impact on the waterfront is that, one way or another, more diversity of activity will appear in Bay Area downtowns and suburban areas, thereby making it possible for (former) commuters to work closer to home—and use the freeway for occasional, rather than frequent, trips. Maybe the inevitable shortage, then exhaustion, of fossil fuels will be the only way to reduce the freeway's traffic, then reduce its size. But many people already consciously rearrange their lives so that they don't have to depend on cars and seldom use freeways. There could be, in other words, a resurgence of grass roots ecological values. Add to that increased public awareness of ecocity principles through education. We could still *choose* to build more sanely, with freeways shrinking, before being forced to cope with a potentially disastrous exhaustion of energy resources. In the long run—50 years plus—the freeway would shrink by design, default, or disaster. We might as well begin planning for that eventuality in a way that sees it as a great opportunity, in a way that makes it as easy as possible to restore the marsh, beach, water circulation, and healthy bayshore life, while adding human uses to a reasonable portion of the land.

The waterfront is here, as in many other cities, a real treasure for the whole community and should be left in a condition that enriches aquatic life and the human spirit. It demands very special treatment. All efforts should be made to shift potential development away from places like Berkeley's once and (I hope) future marsh and toward areas that could sustain it at less ecological cost.

These suggestions have been ignored in the debate up to the time of this writing. The decision-making process has been open and the public has been involved, but it has been a bad process because the assumption throughout has been one of conflict and compromise. There has been little effort to imagine first the best solution and then, armed with a real vision, seek cooperation of all involved. The result of this thinking is that even the Sierra Club, expecting a fight and eventual compromise, is proposing development, if far less than Santa Fe would like, on the marsh—the richest, most ecologically important area of all the land being considered for development. This is land with a thin layer of fill on it presently. It could be left alone until money was found to restore it, first by removal of the fill. It could even become larger than the original marsh to make up for some of the thousands of acres of the Bay that have been filled in the last hundred and fifty years.

If the freeway-side strip development is built, the best we could do is wait until the buildings become rundown in two or three generations, tear them down and start the restoration then. Much larger projects have been demolished—to everyone's benefit. Demolition works but it is expensive, dislocates people, and loses precious time for the bioregion—and the Earth itself. Better to do it right the first time. That way we and our children can enjoy it too.

THE FLATS AND THE HILLS

In Berkeley the lower-income housing is generally on "the Flats" and the higher-income housing is in "the Hills." Both the flat lands and the lower hills of Berkeley were credibly good farm land, though weather was always a bit dry and undependable. In the late 1880s small farms were scattered throughout this area, but over the next thirty or fifty years were replaced by housing and commercial and industrial uses that paid back much more money per acre/effort. The flats ended up as generally lower and moderate income residences, the hills moderate to tastefully splendid with a homey edge. The higher hills, little used for farming, industry, or commerce, provided expensive spectacular views of San Francisco Bay, "the City" (of San Francisco), and the Golden Gate for those that could afford them.

From the 1870s through the 1930s Berkeley developed a network of streets and rail lines, with vehicles evolving from small horse-drawn streetcars to electric streetcars to steam trains, and then devolving to buses to cars—all overlapping temporally with one another until two things happened: The Bay Bridge was completed in 1937 putting an end to ferry service across the bay and most public transportation connecting with the ferry piers. And, second, in 1940 National City (bus) Lines bought up and destroyed the popular electric streetcar system—a conspiracy that brought them a Sherman Anti-Trust Law conviction in 1948. (National City Lines was secretly financed by General Motors, Standard Oil, Firestone Rubber, and Mack Truck and managed to purchase more than 100 urban streetcar systems and switch to buses before they were prosecuted. The bus companies were never planned to be very lucrative—the big money was in selling cars, gasoline, and rubber tires.)

FROM SUBURB TO FARMLAND: A sprawled low-density automobile-dependent area transforms into a farming area and compact, town-sized ecocity. Similar changes could happen in Berkeley and elsewhere in the Bay Area. Through legal devices, tax, loan, and grant incentives; gas and automobile taxes; and other "proximity policies" the city builds up in one area while building down in the out-lying areas. A small compact village appears on the horizon, left flank of the mountain. Time for transition: 50 to 100 years. We're assuming the same population in all three pictures.

Today the great majority of people in both the flats and the hills have cars and are dependent upon them. From the ecocity point of view, the lower densities in both these areas make them ideal for a return to agriculture and nature—not all of them but a significant part. The fact that people in both lower-cost housing and pricy places would be similarly affected takes the issue out of class battle terms and makes the transition potentially quite fair.

The goal of transforming the town into an ecocity is, again, diversity. The strategy requires above all else that residents are well rewarded

---

in the gradual shift from car-dependent scattering to more clustered development.

As private and public funds accumulate (through bonds, state funds, assessment districts, city tax revenues, land bank contributions, etc.) houses along creeks and ridgelines can be removed gradually. Again, clearing buildings should be more than balanced by new development closer to centers. As time goes by and more and more land opens up, lots can be consolidated and little-used streets closed. In the flats substantial home farming and market-crop growing can become established, contributing to healthful fresh food and creating new income-producing work within city limits. In the hills the ridgelines and stream headwaters open up and more natural habitat is re-established. The city could buy two or three hilltop houses, convert them to public use, add more facilities and encourage a restaurant or two, providing cable car access from the North Shattuck neighborhood. Another similar facility could be made accessible from the Elmwood neighborhood, and perhaps a third from downtown through the University campus. Thus certain parts of the ridge would become available to easy public access for sunset watchers while the higher hilly areas, with housing thinning out, would eventually reopen to native vegetation and wildlife.

In both flats and hills many people would choose to stay in place, paying land taxes which would be rising relative to the taxes in the centers. Those that chose to farm and those that stayed to run the public ridge sites would be forgiven part or all of their taxes and would receive other city compensation for their services to the long-term development of the city and its bioregion. But over decades, more and more land would open up, and someday, despite higher populations, the hills would again support many of their original plant and animal species. In the flats, some areas would be similarly transformed while others would produce a sizeable portion of the city's food.

NOW AND IN THE FUTURE: Imagine peeling away the present-day Berkeley to reveal Berkeley 150 years hence. The carpet-like section being lifted off is a portion of Berkeley in the 1980s: averaging one to two story housing with a few scattered apartments, becoming more dense near downtown and neighborhood centers. We are looking east toward Berkeley Hills and the 1980s carpet terminates at approximately Sacramento Avenue, close to the viewer, and Martin Luther King Jr. Way, in the distance. A perpendicular split runs up Cedar Street.

Below, the future is revealed, or at least a far more ecologically

healthy version of it than we could imagine with extention of current
trends. The key features to notice are the clustering of housing and other
mixed uses in centers of larger buildings surrounded by open farm and
natural land. Biology is vastly enriched and natural energy flows taken
advantage of by way of restored creeks, greenhouses, rooftop gardens,
greatly increased solar collectors, wind-electric generators and water
pumps and cisterns for land area, roof run-off. The downtown, right
background, is far denser and taller than in the 1980s with soaring solar
passive architecture glistening in the sun, buildings connected by high-
flying catwalks and bathed in the murmur of human voices and the
gurgling of Strawberry creek, punctuated by sunny stands of fruit trees
and a dark, cool forest of redwoods.

NEIGHBORHOODS

Imagine you are living about five blocks from a neighborhood center. Your next door neighbor's house has come up for sale. Coincidentally, the house next door to hers just suffered a serious fire—not enough to normally require demolition, but since the house had been neglected, has termites and dry rot, the price of repair is approaching replacement cost. Meanwhile an enterprising young urban ecologist has pointed out the double-lot opportunity to the Urban Nature Land Trust. This group buys land and buildings and transfers them to city or non-profit stewardship for future natural or agricultural uses: creeks, hilly slopes, "view sheds," beautiful rock outcroppings, or potential food growing land. The land trust is also bound by its charter to remove housing or workplaces only if replacement spaces are being constructed elsewhere in the city and closer to neighborhood and city centers. Enough money has accumulated in the land trust's coffers from private and public sources that it can make a good offer to both of your neighors, throwing in moving costs and a sum equal to first and last month's rent at comparable places.

The two transactions are completed and within a month the house two doors down is gone. Within six months, the other one is also razed. One household, a single mother and two children, has moved to Walnut Creek where the mother had a job already, to which she would counter-commute every weekday. In the other house lived a man about 50 whose womanfriend and her children had taken to three of the four winds—for work, college, and adventure. He decides it would be nice to live in one of the new low-cost no-car condos. He can walk to work and enjoy views of the Bay Area and downtown from his terrace greenhouse five stories up; he's also within a couple minutes of his

CO·OP PARKING LOT, 1980s

favorite restaurants and the University where he plans to catch a lecture or two and watch a few movies at the Pacific Film Archives every month. He sells his car for $2,000 and discovers that his annual total savings amounts to $3,500, the same figure the American Automobile Association says the average American car owner pays in all car-related costs every year. With this windfall, he takes an annual trip overseas, or via railroad to distant parts of America, Canada, Mexico. Sometimes he rides aboard the exotic new ships with towering metal sails. The new "disposable income," as well as his convenient location, makes it easier for him to become involved in the town's cultural life and helps put his daughter through college.

So you lose these neighbors and you have not one but two vacant lots next door. At first it's weeds hopping with undistinguished sparrows and rasty starlings, occasionally visited by a slinking cat or two. Then one of the urban gardeners from the city's Department of Public Works Urban Agriculture Unit shows up and posts announcements of meetings to plan a program he will coordinate (if a neighbor doesn't volunteer for the job) of running a community/city garden. Depending on response, the city gardener will turn over the land to individuals and small clubs; run it like a city park in which the trimmings are actually food, compost and revenues; or do some mix of the two.

SMALL ELECTRIC CARTS

ADDED HOUSING

EXPANDED CAFE

CO·OP PARKING LOT REVISED
More people live closer and walk. Housing on Bank of America parking lot north of French Hotel. Small vehicles—small parking space.

Five years later three more lots open up on your block. One of them is on the corner next to the home of the man who moved to the no-car condo. On one hand, the old neighborhood is looking a little lonely with vacant spots appearing here and there, fewer cars rushing by. But it is quieter, the view is quite a pleasant surprise, the gardens are beautiful and bountiful and, though you didn't think about such things five years ago, you've begun to really appreciate fresh, locally grown vegetables and fruit, given to you by friends and available at a reasonable price from the Coop. And you've started a tentative garden plot next door yourself, stewarded by a neighborhood volunteer gardener. Composting, coordinated by the same woman, has replaced stinky garbage cans. Those who supply garbage get free compost. Now it's a pleasure to bicycle to downtown on the slow street system. One block toward your neighborhood center you can even float through the new super-slow woonerf, known locally as a foot street; you weave around benches, sculptures, and occasional big trees in the street. Your house is beginning to feel as though it's at the edge of town.

OLD "BUILT-UP" NEIGHBORHOOD CENTER (below dashed line)
AND NEW BUILDING (above line)

Ten years later, there are several more houses missing, a large new orchard of apples, apricots, persimmons, lemons, and various nuts two blocks away, and a newly opened creek less than a block away. You start seeing deer occasionally and at night a distant mooing of cows occasionally mixes with train whistles and fog horns—nights are much quieter now and faraway sounds you used to miss are often audible.

In the other direction, the neighborhood center, just a short walk away, has been built up considerably, yet it has retained a good deal of the local character. A lot more is going on over there. Within a block and a half in each direction of a major intersection the densities are closer to those found in San Francisco neighborhoods but with a mix of Berkeley architectural styles, solar greenhouses, rooftop gardens and shops, and the sort of courtyards, terraces and bridges introduced in the 1970s and 1980s in Walnut Square and the North Shattuck Center. As in many older lively urban neighborhood centers, there are markets of all sorts, hardware stores, Post Office, banks, restaurants, cafes. In the Berkeley tradition there are coops of many kinds, child care centers, clinics and accupressure offices, meeting halls at the thriving Coop food store and in two churches, a synagogue, and a Friends Meeting House. There are also many features and businesses relating directly to the "ecotechnologies" like solar-greenhouse and permaculture design, building and supply companies, and collectives and a

EDIBLE
PINE NUTS

BIOREGION
FLAG
EARTH FLAG
U.S. FLAG

BECAUSE OF BRIDGES AND
ELEVATED PATHWAY, UPPER
LEVELS ARE ACCESSIBLE TO
WHEELCHAIRS WITH FEW
ELEVATORS.

CLOSING STREET, ADDING ALL-WEATHER ARCADES
WITH HOUSING, SHOPS, BUSINESSES ABOVE (heavy lines)

Branch Ecology Center with a neighborhood recycling station.

At this point, you are assessing not only changes in your city but in your own situation. A new flexibility becomes part of your life. Your small savings, house-equity build-up, and years of acquired professional skills and skills from involvements in your community give you new options you didn't think much about before. Your city has new options you never anticipated, as its diversity has increased these ten years.

Now imagine you live in an area adjacent to the neighborhood center. In the first five years a few home owners take advantage of new proximity loans, reduced taxes, and zoning and codes to lift their houses half a story while putting bedrooms in the attic and new units in the basements. These buildings retain their local feel, echoes of Victorian styles, brown shingles, pitched roofs and bay windows, but often with solar greenhouses—even large compost bins—designed into the lines of the house. Assistance from the city's "Ag Unit" and trees from the annual Arbor Day buying binges have lined the streets in veritable forests of diverse edibles. Trellises are festooned with kiwi fruit, choyote, raspberries, blackberries, honeysuckle, jasmine, trumpetvine.

Parking lots for local businesses are disappearing. A few apartments are being built on the same land, some parking lots are turning into

---

parks with playgrounds, community gardens, benches, sculptures. . . .
The parking lots at two of the Coop food stores have been reduced
to half size and, at Cedar and Shattuck, a beautiful garden is enjoying
its first spring. The open-air flower vendors, after years of business,
are selling the first flowers actually grown at their corner. Tables from
the cafe at the French Hotel and Cedar Center spill out onto the park.
Business people, originally fearful that reduced parking would slash
profits, have discovered that some people did stop coming: drivers from
fifteen and forty miles away, also a few from the hills of Kensington,
El Cerrito, and Orinda. But many new people have arrived, some by
bus, some by bike, and some by moving into the area and just walking
over. Some visit who plain love the ambiance of the whole area.

With the slow streets system spreading, many more people are using bicycles and growing numbers are going shopping in small electric
carts. For these vehicles, parking lots feature space and maneuvering
room less than one half as large as those used by conventional cars
serving the same number of shoppers. Growing use of bicycles—and
feet—reduces parking area even more while increasing the number of
people served.

So your neighborhood is busier with people, but quieter—there
are less cars, and they have self-consciously quiet mufflers—the air is
slightly cleaner (though the new trees and flowers make it smell fresher).
After all, the regional situation hasn't changed too much for the better yet. The suburbs continue to spread out and San Francisco and
Oakland are still building office buildings and only just now beginning to think about regional land uses and notice their causal relationship to the traffic jams commuters continually bitch about. The commuters are making more smog and still voting for widening freeways,
and for big parking lots at BART. They're voting against gasoline taxes
that could help support transit.

Another ten years later your neighborhood center is so lively it
sports two tiny movie theaters and a band-stand where people listen
to live music. An increase in public life begins to parallel a decrease
in T.V. watching; doing and participating replacing watching and
vegetating. Now, between the larger buildings, there are bridges across
the street—for pleasure and convenience, not for avoiding traffic—
third-story cafes, rooftop public gardens. Automobile driving has fallen
away so much that streets like Shattuck Avenue have been closed to
traffic. Yet streets like Oxford and Martin Luther King Jr. Way, both
with electric streetcars, carry less auto traffic than in the 1980s. In

a few places—Shattuck, College, Solano, Adeline, Hearst, and Euclid Avenues—the street is covered for a short distance in winter, open in summer. Awnings are the least provision shops give to the public for the rainy season—many have built covered arcades over sidewalks, some with more shops or housing overhead.

A cable-car terminal is a short walk from your house. About once a month you take it to the Summit Center to relax, look out over the Bay Area, show visitors around, and set out upon walks around Tilden Park, to Lawrence Hall of Science or the University of California Botanical Gardens. The reintroduced streetcars are as popular as they were in the 1920s and 1930s before National City Lines bought them up and destroyed them.

On your street, many houses glint and sparkle on the south side with solar greenhouses. At night bicycle headlights glide up and down the streets like streams of fireflies. Car drivers are treated with near contempt on all but major arterials. If they get pushy, a swarm of bicyclists and pedestrians converge, pounding their fists on fenders and rooftops. It's gone that far!

DOWNTOWN

Ironically in a time when overall population needs to shrink, downtown
and urban activity areas need to grow—while sprawl areas go back to
nature and agriculture.

Berkeley, sometimes cheerfully called the People's Republic of
Berkeley by its own citizens, is a promising place to try to accomplish
this. Many Berkeleyans see themselves as citizens of the world, people
of conscience, education, and action. There are jokes around town
about the city's foreign policy and who's going to be Secretary of State
after the next election. In fact, the city was the first to divest in South
Africa (1979) and has sister cities in Nicaragua and on the "other"
side in El Salvador. Through its numerous writers, students, artists,
and political thinkers, Berkeley has long been a major exporter of
valuable new ideas. It has a high level of ecological consciousness:
almost everyone is a member of one environmental group or another,
recycles or composts, hikes in mountain or coastal wildernesses, and
has friends around the world. Berkeley's congressional representative
Ron Dellums has said many times, "What is our policy about after
all? It is about *life*. The bomb is an equal opportunity destroyer. . . . We
must stop the arms race. It is the destruction of *life* to eliminate help
to the poor and elderly, to poison our rivers and oceans. . . . " And,
Berkeley is a comparatively affluent and highly educated community—in
order words, it can afford to try out changes and it should be smart
enough to make the right ones.

If ever there were a city to shoulder the responsibility to experiment with reshaping city structure to heal the Earth and revitalize its
people, Berkeley is a good bet.

For Berkeley, the responsibility to grow means considerable increase

---

in residential growth in and near downtown and continued, though smaller, expansion in commerce and business.

As part of an officially adopted ecocity program the City Council should encourage growth rates one or two percentage points above the regional average for five or ten years, while strictly linking this policy with other ecocity policies. Growth promoted, yes, but only if it contributes to balanced diversity, progressively reduces car-dependence, and incorporates alternatives, conserves energy, and enriches biological diversity. The challenge will thus be laid down to other cities in the region to adopt similar policies. The result of this would be hopefully a sharing of responsibility to reconsider land uses and reshape cities, eventually resulting in dramatic reduction of commuting, energy use, and pollution, and leading to better land uses. The Association of Bay Area Governments and the Metropolitan Transportation Commission, the regional planning agencies for the Bay Area cities and counties, could be inspired and goaded to take greater responsibility for promoting ecocity development patterns.

After a few years, regional and local progress could be assessed by the city of Berkeley, and strategy could be amended according to experience. The effect, if any, on city governance and development worldwide could also be carefully monitored.

Parking policy is crucial to ecocity changes in all downtowns including Berkeley's. New parking should be frozen, then reduced year by year. Inside parking at $15,000 to $30,000 per space, plus added traffic control costs, represent gigantic investments in environmental degradation; if invested in alternatives—slow streets, better transit, pedestrian amenities, bicycle facilities, and above all else, mixed use planning and supportive "proximity policies"—the ecological consequences would be equally far-reaching, but healthy rather than pathological. The waste of space in cheaper open-air parking is as damaging environmentally as the waste of money in sheltered parking: it spreads buildings and people farther apart, making pedestrian access more difficult, inconvenient. Parking lots are large holes in the urban fabric, subtly diluting social and commercial vitality. A parking lot here and there goes unnoticed but the cumulative effect is a significant expansion of the surface area of downtown and proportionally more walking, more fatigue and fewer contacts in a day's activity.

One of the most environmentally damaging acts of Berkeley's recent city government was to establish for the first time *requirements* to build parking along with new development. Until 1984 developers

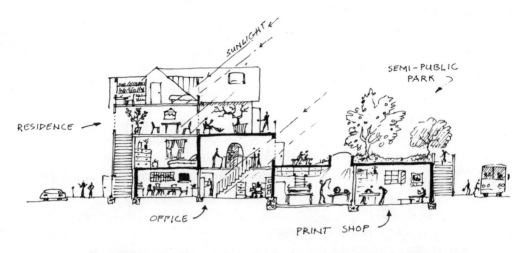

CHANGING A PARKING STRUCTURE TO OTHER USES

One of an infinite number of possibilities is shown here with parking displaced by a three story residence, an office, a print shop and a semi-public park. The floor was lowered in the print shop to make higher ceilings and a diffuse light skylight was added for natural lighting. Notice that the trees are placed close to the posts where support is best. The office has a second story interior balcony; the residence has a south-facing patio where someone reading in the sun is about to be joined by a friend. Buses (and shoes), rather than cars, carry most of the people in their comings and goings.

were allowed to build parking. Now they are forced to build it. In the ecologically healthy city downtown they will not even be allowed to insert such damaging tissue into the city's living body.

Instead of places for cars to gather—parking lots—we should build places where people gather: homes, parks, gardens, bus stops, train stations. . . . As people switch from car to bicycle and—for those that need them—all-weather electric carts, considerable acreage opens up for other uses.

Preferential parking around city centers is a good interim phase, allowing residents to park on their streets while other drivers begin to figure out strategies for getting into these areas without driving a car, except when unavoidable. In areas adjacent to downtown and major centers, say within three or four blocks—that is, a short walk—larger buildings should be encouraged. There's no reason why these buildings have to be ugly, simple boxes offering slab-like walls to the public view, unless the plan is to paint murals on them. The local styles could be used and amended. Some good examples are in the South Campus area. The six-story Berkeley Women's City Club at 2315 Durant designed by Julia Morgan with its tile roof, tower, courtyard, sixth-floor bridges is an example; the Bernard Maybeck house at 2401 Dwight at Dana, with its wide spanning eaves; Fenwick Weavers' Village and Roachdale Village of the University Students Cooperative Association on the same block, with fourth- and third-story bridges, solar hot water, rooftop patios, and ground-level courtyards and its own small park; the old brick hotels on Telegraph Avenue; the sunny back courtyard, now Reza's Garden Restaurant, surrounded by four- to six-story apartments; and the hundreds of two- and three-story houses with basement and/or attic units, making the buildings effectively three to five stories of living, useful space.

The future downtown could enlarge these patterns, adding housing while emphasizing commercial, entertainment, and educational uses, and adding greenhouses, rooftop, and terrace gardens, all of which could complement local styles or lead in new aesthetic directions. Rooftop uses that are hard to justify financially on a small building, are more economical if the building is larger. Roofs can be sealed and covered with earth, as they are on the Graduate Theological Union classrooms in Northside, which are covered with grass lawns. Kaiser Center in Oakland has had a five-story parking lot with a 3-1/2 acre rooftop garden complete with small lake since 1960. More diminutive versions could open up beautiful new private and public spaces on larger neighborhood and downtown buildings.

With less traffic, several streets in the downtown could be closed to all vehicles and several to all but buses. Strawberry Creek could run right through downtown; where streets pass over the creek, we could remove parking to keep the street as narrow as possible and the creek as correspondingly open. Urban fruit and nut trees could march along the street sides and up islands right through downtown and out into the neighborhoods and farmlands of the flats. New, nearly-silent streetcars, low and easy to get in and out of, would zip in and out of the area while BART would continue to connect Berkeley with other urban centers.

Some streets would be partially covered in the rainy season with fantastic structures looking a little like the crystal palaces of the 1800s, perhaps like the greenhouse garden at the Courthouse on the Pacific Garden Mall of Santa Cruz. Many buildings would be connected by bridges—two small, simple and very attractive examples of which are presently located at the Cedar Center between the main and west buildings. Sidewalk cafes would bustle with human sounds, rather than automotive sounds, and the air would be as fresh as downwind-from-Bay-Area auto grids and arteries permit. Pedestrian passages would cut through blocks, and refurbished alleyways would create intimate-scale access in most of the downtown. Trumpetvine Court is an example of this today and if many of the business people in downtown have their way, more such passages will be built with or without other elements of ecocity planning. Thus the precedent of Berkeley's very unusual and beautiful system of walks and steps bisecting residential blocks in the hills and scattered locations on the flats could be reflected in the downtown.

In this vision, shadows of rooftop windmills flicker on the streets here and there; reflected sunlight bounces between greenhouses and office buildings. Transparent prism aqueducts cast rippling spectral colors across cafe umbrellas as they carry part of Strawberry Creek through town in a series of living fish ladder sculptures and gravity fountains. The downtown sounds are of conversation, laughter, breezes in the trees, water flowing, birds singing. . . .

In Berkeley, as in many other cities, there are many environmentalists and some people who think of themselves as ecologists who are dead set against tall buildings. Height limit discussions are always hot around the collar at public hearings on downtown planning, with developers and business people fudging upward and neighborhood activists, preservationists, earthier types, and weekend wilderness lovers fudging downward. Berkeley should put the criteria of community and ecological health above all other criteria and see what results. Since centers need to grow as fringe areas shrink, tall buildings must be considered for Berkeley. As mentioned earlier, creating a sense of comfortableness and calm is only one of the important functions of the city. Tall buildings add diversity and vitality by creating a sense of challenge and by symbolizing and inspiring creative adventure.

Berkeley has a particularly ugly downtown skyline dominated by the Great Western Building, ten stories taller than most of the rest of the buildings and much broader than the second tallest Wells Fargo

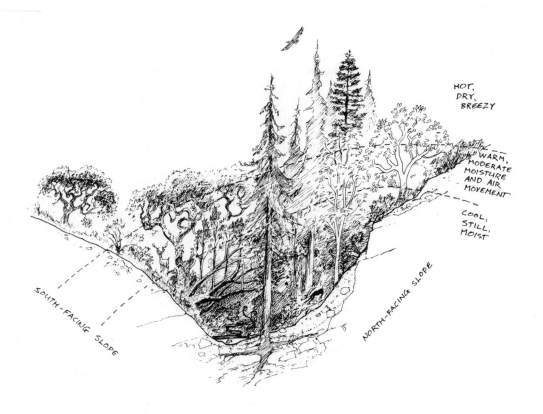

HOT, DRY, BREEZY

WARM, MODERATE MOISTURE AND AIR MOVEMENT

COOL, STILL, MOIST

SOUTH-FACING SLOPE

NORTH-FACING SLOPE

MICROCLIMATES IN HIGH-DENSITY NATURAL AREAS AND ECOCITIES

Where trees and buildings block sun and air movement, the microclimate is generally much cooler and more moist. Tall buildings are often said to "cause" windy streets. But this is no more true than saying redwood trees, the tallest in nature, cause windy canyons. In fact, the stillness at the base of these giants is almost spooky sometimes. The relationship between buildings and streets—and open parking lots and parks—and the direction of the winds relative to the layout of the streets determines whether the streets are swept by the wind or not.

Above, a typical creek and canyon environment in the East Bay with more vegetation on the north-facing slope. Opposite, an "urban edge" with a high-density, high-diversity town center meeting a high-density, high-diversity natural landscape. This is like the meeting of two downtowns, the cultural and the natural. Notice the cafe whose sign letters are metal wind chimes, the sculptural fish ladder and plexiglas prism aqueduct which carry part of the local creek through town amid shimmering rainbow swatches and refreshing splashes and gurglings. There are murals on the sides of some buildings, and the rooftop headquarters of the Earth Party flies one of its various child-designed Earth Flags. The bridges are schematic. Then again,

HOT,
DRY,
BREEZY

COOLER,
WETTER,
MORE STILL...
DEPENDING
ON DIRECTION
OF WIND

if we don't burn up all our fossil "fuels" perhaps one day we will be able to devise super-strong transparent materials to add this element of adventure and spectacle to our towns.

Building across the street. Tearing down such a large building would be absurdly expensive and counter to the density-shift trends that are needed for healthier cities. A solution to the aesthetic problem harmonious with ecocity principles would be to allow several buildings taller than the Great Western Building, requiring that there is a proportional increase in housing and decrease in office space for the combined downtown and immediately adjacent neighborhood. If buildings are approved on a one at a time basis on mixed use criteria, if they have to incorporate such features as bridge connections to other buildings, solar heating and cooling, and must also provide funds for slow streets and transit, if they additionally are required to provide transit passes and bike lockers instead of parking places for cars and if they do not exceed any previous building heights by more than 20%, then they should be permitted.

Tall buildings could, in a sense, reflect the tall redwoods of the area, once common in the valleys and on the lower north slopes of hills. It would be appropriate, then, to incorporate a redwood grove right in the middle of downtown, perhaps eliminating Center Street between Shattuck and King Way, allowing the towering trees to march down the street past City Hall, on its north side, with Strawberry Creek flowing by to the south. The creek and lawns and small stands of fruit trees in the park would be bathed in sun. It would be like walking from a sun-baked grassy hill of the Northern California coast into a cool, dark redwood canyon; the downtown redwood grove would create a towering, cool canyon of living columns to the north of several major buildings. Just around the corner would be the warm, sunny orchard, creek, and lawn area. Workers on the 12th floor of the Great Western Building would then look north into the massive branches—of course these would take a long time to grow—and the trees would eventually tower over the building, obscuring its homely waffle-like facade, maybe out-living the building by a thousand years. They would grow slowly, in the same spirit in which the cathedrals were built over hundreds of years—in dedication to the deepest future.

The economic development of downtown could have several major themes based on bioregional conditions and the city's unique history. The University would continue to be a mainstay of employment and secondary services. The industrial activity in West Berkeley would continue. South Berkeley commercial activity would grow several times over. Rebuilding the city itself with a strong emphasis on downtown would be a major undertaking generating many jobs, and since this revitalization would constitute an ecocity prototype, it could be partially financed by outside sources of investment and occasional research and development grants. With recovery of streams and marshes, fishing could make a comeback, adding its daily catch to the restaurant business. And finally, a major slice of the new economic action could lead to "serious tourism" with people coming to the city to see how the transitions are going, studying ecocity changes, enjoying downtown's sidewalk cafes beside the creek, participating in the festivals on the solstices and equinoxes, learning from the world-wide influences that converge at this home of one of the world's finest universities and across the bay from one of the world's most beautiful cities—now experiencing stiff competition from its exuberant little sister on the eastern bayshore.

CITY HALL, LOOKING EAST

With a redwood mini-forest to the north, fruit trees and creek to the south and west, and a solar heat-collecting "trombe wall" on the south side of the building, changes in Berkeley City Hall and its landscaping would express a commitment to an ecologically healthy and diverse future. In the background are new buildings with rooftop gardens, greenhouses, and bridges between buildings. The leaf-shaped tower has greenhouse terraces on the south—open in summer, closed in winter—and offices on the north.

TRANSPORTATION

Land use determines transportation needs, as mentioned several times now. Berkeley has a headstart toward an ecocity transportation solution since it is fairly diverse in its land uses and the mix generally places different uses close to one another: "access by proximity, not transportation."

Some have suggested, like Hazel Henderson, that transportation is a measure of social dysfunction, and certainly where it is dominated by automobiles this is accurate. But some modes of getting about are fun to many people, like bicycling, walking, taking ferries or streetcars—"rolling architecture," as designer/writer Christopher Swan calls them—and some modes are outright healthy, like bicycling and walking—unless you are stuck breathing auto exhaust or struck by a steel fender.

In Berkeley, in recognition of these observations and for other reasons, a bicycle plan was initiated in the early 1970s and a slow street concept introduced in the early 1980s. An assessment district to fund these and other downtown projects is under discussion in 1986. The first slow street, Milvia Street from University Avenue to Cedar Street, was funded by mitigation money from a large development, Golden Bear Center, at the corner of University and Milvia. The money is to be used to mitigate traffic impacts caused by the development, specifically for slow streets and several other traffic control measures. In the future, mitigation charges, sometimes in the form of "transportation services fees," could be required of all new large developments in the city, each major project paying for a new stretch of slow street until the whole city is served by a network of safe, pleasant streets where the bicycle has priority over the car. These same funds can be used to support the local bus company directly, as is done in San Fran-

---

cisco, or by helping employers subsidize transit passes for employees. They can also be disbursed in outright cash grants to people who walk and bike to work, since each such person can save the employer thousands of dollars per parking space avoided. Employees of Palo Alto's City government are now paid 5¢ per mile for business travel on their bicycles and 35¢ per mile when they take their car. This tiny start of a good thing could end up with, say, 50¢ per mile for bikes and nothing for cars.

Some of the transportation services money could also go into a fund to make money available for building housing nearer to the jobs—a mitigation at the very source of the problem. Such "crossover funding" could have profound impact. Imagine if gasoline tax money crossed over from the transportation sector to the construction sector for building housing that didn't require the automobile.

Streetcars and buses are beneficial for all the reasons so often cited in these pages and should be important in connecting Berkeley's activity centers and downtown with others in the Bay Area. Taxis for getting around occasionally and rental cars for travel into the country or to car-dependent areas are far superior to privately owned cars because there needs to be only a small fraction as many of them; the less the total number of cars, the healthier the city, bioregion, and planet. The more the city is structured around access by proximity, the weaker the Auto Sprawl Syndrome, the more practical the taxi and rent-a-car option becomes.

BART (Bay Area Rapid Transit commuter rail line) deserves special comment. It was originally conceived to connect downtown San Francisco, and to a lesser degree, downtown Oakland, to the suburbs. As it developed and spread it remained true to that dubious vision of uniting sprawl with single-use downtowns. Conspicuous evidence of this is seen in its large parking areas near stations in suburbs and in low-density areas of cities as "built up" as Berkeley. These parking lots are being greatly expanded in 1986 and '87 at a cost of tens of millions of dollars. New land is being acquired and, in Berkeley, landscaping is being removed for yet more cars.

BART's philosophy will have to change if the Bay Area is to be served by urban trains in an ecologically healthy manner. The idea has to be service between large and medium sized urban centers, not service between parking lots and urban centers. In Berkeley at the Ashby BART station that means parking should be removed, at the rate of several dozen spaces a year, and replaced by bicycle and small cart parking and eventually most of the land should be sold off for higher-density uses.

At the North Berkeley Station, badly located in the first place, four blocks of low-density housing were cleared for a large parking lot. Instead of being enlarged that lot should be slowly reduced in size and eventually torn up for farming. When it is about one third of its present size, say in ten or fifteen years, the station should be closed altogether. Albany, just a mile and a half north, decided it didn't want a BART station, though it has a sizeable activity center near the point where BART crosses Solano Avenue. A station should be located there, with new housing and jobs developing in the immediate area and *no* new parking provided for the train other than small cart and bicycle parking.

In 1975 Fremont, at the south end of the BART line in the East Bay, rezoned the area within 1/2 mile of its BART station for higher-density housing, purposefully providing a "place" to coordinate with the "route." Very simple, very reasonable—and eleven years later, despite intense original skepticism, very successful.

Carpools and van pools, fairly popular in Berkeley, are a little better than single occupant cars, but not by much since they still connect sprawl with work place and thus perpetuate the land uses that *cause* the urban transportation problem. Carpools save gas and reduce pollution relative to driving cars alone, but, like solar collectors in suburbia, may serve to make people think they are doing a lot to help when in fact the positive contribution is far smaller than the damage caused by the related land uses. "Casual carpooling" in the morning is having a disastrous effect on A.C. Transit, the local bus company, costing thousands of dollars in lost revenues every day. In order to speed through the toll bridge to San Francisco in the free (no charge) carpool lane, drivers pirate passengers away from bus stops around the East Bay, depositing them at the bus terminal in downtown San Francisco. Since these workers live in scattered locations they can't catch informal carpool rides in the other direction, and so, they take the bus one way, forcing the bus company to run underutilized buses into San Francisco and full ones out in the evening. Thus, these commuters demonstrate another way in which even the carpool automobile has a damaging effect.

Berkeley can do little about the massive freeway that rumbles along its shoreline, ruining the mouths of its creeks and destroying its beaches and marshes while casting its pollution onto gardens for blocks, and

ELEVATED STREET

An elevated foot and bicycle path passes through a compact downtown of considerable diversity. The slopes and crowns of the surface of the elevated path takes rain water to planters along its edges—no other irrigation necessary. Many, but not all buildings, take advantage of the sun's angle to the south (right). A subway is under the street level. A forest meets town on the south edge. The elevated path connects with another high-density town center two or three miles away creating a destination for a beautiful ride or walk, partially through the treetops and branches and partially at ground level.

RAIN WATER RUNS TO PLANTERS

into lungs for miles down wind. People who don't like the freeway and its massive impacts traditionally throw up their hands in political impotence with the traditional noisy kicking and screaming, and far from making slow inroads against the giant mechanized rattlesnake, stand by ineffectually while lane after lane is added: two more scheduled for 1987.

Berkeley can do little to affect the freeway other than become an example of new land use patterns—and that's *a lot! Then* maybe Berkeley can help convince regional and state agencies and other cities that sprawl and long distance urban driving can be reduced. In time, sprawling new developments may form new town nuclei with their own jobs or else disband for nearby cities or more distant towns and villages. Then San Francisco might build housing in significant excess of new work places. Then trains will become more popular between cities at long distance, and BART will thrive while providing a service for medium distances appropriate to ecological health. Then the freeway can start to quiet down, lanes can be removed and it can assume smaller, less destructive proportions. Then bicycle and foot paths can cross it with relative ease and for reasonable construction expense. Then maybe we could even afford to put much of it underground as at Freeway Park in Seattle, Washington, under land uses connecting West Berkeley with the Marina and shoreline.

But perhaps the most exhilarating, just plain fun new transportation feature would be the one with the highest visibility, literally: the bridges linking public places three and six stories above ground level in downtown, West Berkeley, and South Berkeley. With soaring views in all directions, we'd have the first inklings of a kind of grounded flight to be experienced in larger ecocities of the future, a mix of relatively high-tech construction with rich biological systems supported by sun, wind, and water energy, nurtured organically and maintained largely with recycled materials—a new world connected by stairs, escalators, elevators, bridges, and good old walking. Berkeley is probably too small scale to incorporate bicycles above ground level, but eventually the foot bridges between buildings of the next decade or two could lead toward bicycle paths in the sky in thirty or forty years in larger centers. In Amsterdam in the late 60s an organization called the Provos placed free "White Bikes" around town: just pick up a bike, pedal to your destination and leave it on the street for the next person. It was a moderately successful extemporaneous transportation system that broke down eventually for lack of continued maintenance. In the ecocity of the future there could be city-owned and maintained white bikes on ground level, blue on the the third level, yellow on the sixth. . . .

Between cities? With stronger centers, less sprawl, and less dependence on cars, we could revive the ferries to San Francisco, which would, along with the developing village of small islands and and canals at the Marina, increase east-west movement on University Avenue to the point that A.C. Transit service there would at last be frequent and efficient. As in the forties and early fifties, the trip from Shattuck and University in downtown to San Francisco would be faster on the bus, then ferry, than it is in the 1980s on the BART—and far more pleasurable, with coffee, coctails, beer and wine, snacks, card games or fog, sea breezes and salt spray to fit the traveler's mood. Between

ENERGY-CONSERVING TRANSPORT

Important urban vehicles of the future: delivery vans, so that shoppers don't need to carry heavy or bulky packages home from the store, and shopping carts. In Berkeley, hundreds of grocery buyers carry their food home in shopping carts, leaving the empty carts on the sidewalk in front of their houses—an effective and simple alternative to driving for people who live within about six blocks of a food market. A cart collection service retrieves the carts with a pick up truck for a fee paid by the grocery store, and sometimes shoppers walk them back to the store when they come across them on the street. The system could be formalized: shoppers could be encouraged to take carts home and leave them just off the sidewalk, and they could be encouraged to walk them back to the store when headed in that direction. The stores could provide a surplus of carts and the city could help by shifting a small portion of money from street repair and traffic control budgets to cart subsidies, thus cutting down on traffic, reducing the number of parking places required at stores and eliminating the only real necessity some people have for owning a car.

ecocities, instead of being anchored to your car seat, you freely walk about the new solar trains, enjoying conversation in the lounge cars and meals in the dining cars, or you take in the expansive views of a landscape becoming ever richer in wildlife, small farms, and occasional new villages. Or you watch the moon reflecting off the metal sails of the new ships on coastal voyages. For longer distances you take the big jets already common in the 1970s and 1980s—when fully loaded they are fairly energy efficient. You can use the outside lane (closed to motor vehicles) of the much quieter freeways to practically fly your wind bike with its transparent sail downwind to your destination, pedaling only when the wind is in front. Many things become possible when we build ecocities.

ENERGY

Much good work has been done on energy conservation in Berkeley and around the world by this time: insulation, cogeneration, solar water and air heating, passive and active systems, with or without solar greenhouses. . . . All are well worked out on the one-building-at-a-time level and instruction and guides are easily available at any library or bookstore. Berkeley's Residential Energy Conservation Ordinance and the law allowing solar greenhouses to cross setback lines are good steps, and recycling—which saves energy—is working fairly well thanks to the Ecology Center, other groups, and general citizen support. The Energy and Resources Group on the University Campus is a major resource. Regionally, geothermal and wind energy make significant contributions to electricity supply and a growing awareness of renewable energy sources, thanks to the efforts of Berkeley-based Environmental Defense Fund and other organizations. Pacific Gas and Electric, the regional energy utility, produces more than 50% of the California wind-generated electricity at Altamont pass about 30 miles from Berkeley. This is the world's largest "wind farm."

What's missing? A consciousness of how enormously negative the automobile and sprawled land uses are, and a consciousness of how to rebuild the city for energy conservation and automobile-independence, that is, freedom from auto-dependence.

Some 72% of all residential energy use is related to transportation and the compact/diversity vs. sprawl/uniform use issue, says solar architect and planner Peter Calthorpe. The most important thing any city could do in regard to energy is to radically curtail automobiles while concentrating and diversifying activity centers. The future Berkeley may glisten and twinkle with sun and stars glancing off solar collectors and windmill propellers, but if it reshapes itself to eliminate dependence on the automobile, it will have made the greatest contribution to energy conservation and energy *understanding* in this century.

NUT TREE SHAKER AT WORK

FOOD AND WOOD

Berkeley's food resources are considerable, and crops can thrive year round in its mild climate. Long term forestry could mix utility with amenity. The bounty of the Bay would again be very significant if creeks and marshes were restored and if state and regional agencies worked to clean up and restore fresh water inflow coming into the San Francisco Bay.

There are many routes to a more bountiful Berkeley. Opening up land by clustering the city on smaller land areas is indispensable. Streets can be made narrower as easily as they can be made wider—departments of public works routinely call for street widenings in many cities. We should call for the opposite with the same assumption, that if the public good is at stake, no problem—just do it. Rooftops can add garden space too, though obviously not as much as by opening up actual land surface. Smaller, less chemical-, energy- and transportation-dependent farms will be the agricultural vanguard of a healthy future. It would be ironic (if appropriate—since most eaters live there) if cities rather than rural areas were to pioneer this small-scale agriculture. Cities like Berkeley could have their own Departments of Agriculture as they now have their Parks and Recreation Departments—which grow plenty of decorative lawns, hedges and trees on public parks and trim private street-side trees. The Departments' motto could be "The greatest fine art of the future will be the making of a comfortable living from a small piece of land"—Abraham Lincoln. Its responsibility would be helping people grow their own and putting city land into cultivation for both food and wood that can't be practically cultivated privately.

To back up the Agriculture Department effort, new zoning and codes are required. Goats and pigs should be legalized in certain areas

---

of Berkeley, cows and other animals later when plots of land are larger. At present, chickens, rabbits, and bees are accepted. Fruit and nut street trees should be legalized, their maintenance, care, and harvesting guaranteed. Private and community gardens and gardens for apartment dwellers and home owners, from window box size to an acre or more, for personal use or public sale should all be encouraged and gardeners should be provided with information and free or low-cost compost.

In food production, as well as energy alternatives, Berkeley has a headstart over many communities. Several home gardeners make a good living on tiny acreage selling specialty lettuce and vegetables to gourmet restaurants in town. This market could be steadily expanded to a larger clientele as more land comes under cultivation. Woods, especially valuable hardwoods, could be planted for high quality lumber production in the long term future: a gift to our children to compensate somewhat for our theft of the fossil fuels. Some fast-growing fuel wood could be planted for a much earlier harvest. The Chinese have been harvesting trees planted in their cities since their Revolution.

In Berkeley, the University, the botanical gardens, the Conservation and Resources Studies school, and the citizens presently involved in gardening and permaculture all contribute in their own unique ways. The genetic engineers say they have high-tech ways to breed biological control agents to limit pests; on one hand, presenting the vision of a world relieved of chemical pesticides; on the other, raising the specter of mutant bugs, microscopic or otherwise, rampaging out of the East Bay like demons from Pandora's box. Others headquartered in Berkeley, notably Integrated Pest Management/Associates, using intricate ecological knowledge, promote biological pest control via subtle manipulation of existing natural or non-toxic chemical means, with recourse to chemicals and toxics in special cases.

The great agricultural debate, then, is rumbling around under Berkeley's urban camouflage already. In the late nineteen thirties and early forties the Manhattan Project was administered from the University of California, Berkeley, as are Los Alamos, Sandia, and Livermore nuclear and "Star Wars" research and development projects today. Bringing the great agricultural debate to the forefront in connection with ecocity transformation may one day be as important a part of Berkeley's destiny as the atomic bomb—and with ramifications equally as momentous and, hopefully, far more auspicious.

THE UNIVERSITY

The University of California should join with the city in taking a leading role in ecocity development—in two ways: by example in its own growth, and by establishing a School of Ecocity Design.

Continued expansion of the University has been a raw spot in "town and gown" relations. Instead of anger, the reaction of the city government and the citizens should be an insistence that growth be along ecocity lines, that if any new facility is built on campus, twice as much student and faculty and staff housing must be provided by the University either on campus or within, say, three blocks.

The University presently provides carpooling for staff and students—a fair start. In addition, the University should take an assertive role in discouraging students and staff from bringing cars to Berkeley. Parking costs should start to increase rapidly. Soon after, parking spaces, then entire parking lots, should be removed to return open space to campus and adjacent areas or to provide for new building—housing first.

The parking lots between Tolman Hall and the Biochemistry Building in the northwest corner of campus should be removed as soon as possible and an eight to ten story, highly complex set of interconnected buildings should be constructed there as the facilities for the new School of Ecocity Design. These buildings would include the housing for twice as many students as planned to be enrolled in the School of Ecocity Design. There would be narrow streets between them, rooftop gardens, and cafes with views over the entire Bay Area. Solar greenhouses and passive design, plenty of insulation and thermal mass would be provided. People could walk the streets between the buildings and take the rooftop-level bridges from one building to another and all the way into downtown or diagonally across the street to the cultivated fields of the Oxford Agricultural Tract. Or people could bicycle out of the complex, across campus and into the city's slow-streets system. The ecocity example would thus be structurally established in the infrastructure of the school and linked to the biological world with its greenhouses and with its bridge to the Oxford tract. And the University itself would be linked to the larger urban community with its bridge to downtown.

The School of Ecocity Design curricula would feature crossdisciplinary studies bringing together elements of urban design and architecture with energy and resources, forestry and agriculture, systems analysis, and peace and conflict resolution studies—to help end the war between our cities and nature.

The state education system would finance construction, and the city would place a high priority on designing and helping to pay for slow streets and bridge connections, open up internships for students and continue cosponsorship of Berkeley TRiP (Transit, Rides and Parking), a program designed to promote "alternatives to the single-occupant car." The School of Ecocity Design would be one of the chief objects of scrutiny and pleasure for the "serious tourists" as well as the students who come to Berkeley for studying what a healthy future might look like—so that they too can participate in helping to build it.

ROOFTOP CAFE, SCHOOL OF ECOCITY DESIGN

The building on the left, foreground, has a solar greenhouse on the south side. The building with the rooftop cafe has a trombe wall on the south side: a dark colored wall covered with glass and vented so that the sun's warmth is captured and transfered to the air inside the building. Foot bridges connect with Mulford Hall, center and left middleground, Warren Hall, extreme right, and downtown across Oxford Street, right background. The silhouette of the hawk on the glassed-in bridge between the Ecocity Design School buildings prevents birds from crashing into the glass. Coffee: Peet's 101 blend.

ECOLOGY PEACE CENTER

Another of the important shrines for the pilgrims seeking a vision of balance between nature and culture, and between societies would be the Ecology Peace Center. Berkeley's deep involvement in war-and-peace and social-justice issues and its role as an innovator in the environmental and appropriate technology movements requires that a special place be built to focus on this history—and to conjure visions for a better future.

Every city should have a place where the meaning of its own unique history can be examined and every city should have a place where its people come to share visions and thoughts of their common destiny, in relation to their bioregion, country, and world.

In Berkeley, there happens to be an ideal place for such a special use. It's the northwest corner of the landfill, the old garbage dump on the Bay. On this site a museum and peace-and-ecology center could house changing exhibitions portraying the world movement for peace and environmental recovery, featuring Berkeley's special relationship to it. Built on a peninsula of garbage reaching out deep into the bay, a public space on this site would do homage to recycling and celebrate the striking views to the Golden Gate and beyond, a place from which to reach out to the world, a place to receive the ocean wind in your teeth and accept ideas from the outside world.

The building should be large enough for major exhibitions but not out of scale for this medium sized town. Display space might amount to about the same area as the University Art Museum on Bancroft or a little less. The structure would be aligned on an axis pointing directly toward the Golden Gate, and the Pacific beyond, toward the great suspension bridge and the rocky ramparts of Marin and San

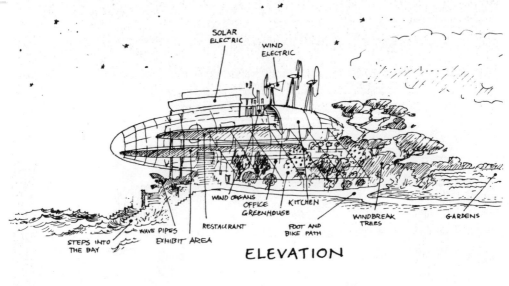

SOLAR ELECTRIC

WIND ELECTRIC

WIND ORGANS
OFFICE
GREENHOUSE

KITCHEN

WINDBREAK TREES

GARDENS

RESTAURANT

FOOT AND BIKE PATH

WAVE PIPES

EXHIBIT AREA

STEPS INTO THE BAY

ELEVATION

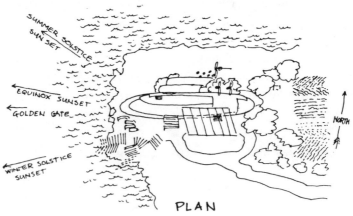

SUMMER SOLSTICE SUN SET

EQUINOX SUNSET

GOLDEN GATE

WINTER SOLSTICE SUNSET

NORTH

PLAN

ECOLOGY/PEACE CENTER/MUSEUM

Francisco—not a bad symbol for a beautiful intertwining of the natural and human-built environments. The arching south side of the building and ceiling should be of tempered (earthquake-safe) glass and steel, with solar greenhouse attached, the north side well insulated and punctuated with portals that would line up with the sunset and sunrise points of the solstice and equinoxes. Markings on the floor would describe these points and tell, with your shadow, the time of day, like a sun-

The labels within the illustration read: GREENHOUSE, EXHIBITIONS, RESTAURANT, KITCHEN, OFFICE, SHOP, ← SOUTH

**INTERIOR, LOOKING WEST,
ECOLOGY/PEACE CENTER/MUSEUM**

dial. In this way the museum/center could be firmly located in Earth, time, and place.

Heat and electricity would be from the sun and wind. Farms would be tilled immediately adjacent, and crops grown in the greenhouse. A restaurant on a balcony would look down to one side on the exhibition area and out to the city of San Francisco and the Golden Gate, the Berkeley Hills to the other. Foods featured here would be from the adjacent gardens, from the farms of Berkeley, and from the Bay.

In order to teach about natural cycles, the building could be designed so that the stars overhead would be visible through a glass canopy: the wildlife, the natural history of the area, the experiments at solving ecocity and appropriate technology problems would all be put on display.

The location of such a facility would have another relationship to the content of its displays: in the same county not far away are presently located Livermore Lab where nuclear and Star Wars weapons are designed, and Alameda, home port for the world's largest war ship, the nuclear aircraft carrier Carl Vinson. If the Mayor of San Francisco gets her way, the giant battleship (and its whole "battle group" of destroyers and support ships) called by its detractors "Death Star Missouri" or "the most expensive obsolete propaganda device for promoting war ever recommissioned," will be stationed directly between Berkeley's old dump and the high seas beyond the Golden Gate. Victor Frankl, psychiatrist and author of *Man's Search for Meaning*, has called for the equivalent of a "Statue of Responsibility" on the west coast to balance the Statue of Liberty on the east coast. The site of the Ecology Peace Center would be a perfect location for something in the same spirit.

If the content of the exhibition hall becomes too heavy you can always go outside and sit on the stairs that drop down into the Bay waves, rest among the mussels and sea anemones at low tide, maybe among the sea otters that might return if the creeks and shoreline are restored and the water allowed to heal itself. You could listen to the wind and waves, to wind harps and wave organs designed by Peter Richards from the Exploratorium. What's it all about? Like Ron Dellums said: Life!

One last point about the site and its potential, a point worth considering in these times of an embattled Berkeley Waterfront: the City of Berkeley owns it.

MAPPING OUT AN ECOCITY STRATEGY FOR BERKELEY

To understand how to rebuild Berkeley or any other city as an ecocity it's helpful to look at the area as it was before people arrived. Then we can map out the features that are unique, useful, or of strong meaning to people. In the process we can respect natural features, take note of creeks, shoreline, dangerous places, wind and calm. We can look for unique areas: confluences of creeks, places where diversity of natural features come together, places with beautiful views. Then we can think in terms of building near but not on the most diverse areas, building to add to human diversity while maintaining natural diversity as much as possible, building to *celebrate* the special places.

On Map 1 we see some of the natural features that should be taken into consideration, from the ridgelines (sawtooth line) and steep slopes (diagonal lines), to the windy bayshore (stippled area). These maps are not detailed enough or large enough to include many very important features from the ecocity point of view: springs, beautiful rock out-croppings, magnificent old trees, a particular microenvironment hosting a rare species, an especially lovely meadow, a glade, a section of valley with a striking configuration of hills, slopes, grassy areas. . . . These things are not included here for lack of space, but should be when a serious attempt is to be made at ecocity planning. In many cases, finding such places will require as much historical research as walking about and looking, since cities weren't generally built with much sensitivity and such places were generally covered over or otherwise radically altered. The major features, though, like the ones on this map, should determine the broad outlines of where to build what.

On map 2, select a point that looks like a good place for a downtown center (small dot) and find two, three, or four sub-centers for

---

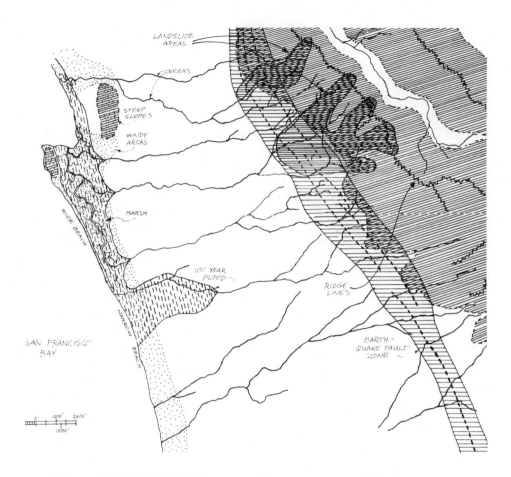

Labels on map: LANDSLIDE AREAS, CREEKS, STEEP SLOPES, WINDY AREAS, MARSH, WIDE BEACH, 100 YEAR FLOOD, RIDGE LINES, NARROW BEACH, SAN FRANCISCO BAY, EARTH- QUAKE FAULT ZONE

Scale: 0 1200' 2400' / 1800'

Map 1. BERKELEY BEFORE EUROPEANS ARRIVED

variety (small triangles).

Then consider where the actual centers of the town are today (medium-sized dot and triangles). Select revised centers that strike a compromise between the ideal and the actual major centers (large dot and large triangles). These points will be centers for five concentric circles that will become the guidelines for ecocity zoning. Locate existing neighborhood centers for similar concentric circles.

The underlying concept behind drawing these circles is simply that distance requires energy and time to traverse. The greater the distance people have to travel, the higher the use of resources and the greater the production of pollution and waste of time. Therefore, we should build relatively compact centers. These areas will then work well with any public transit connecting them to other relatively high-use areas. Within and between the spots of higher activity people can find it

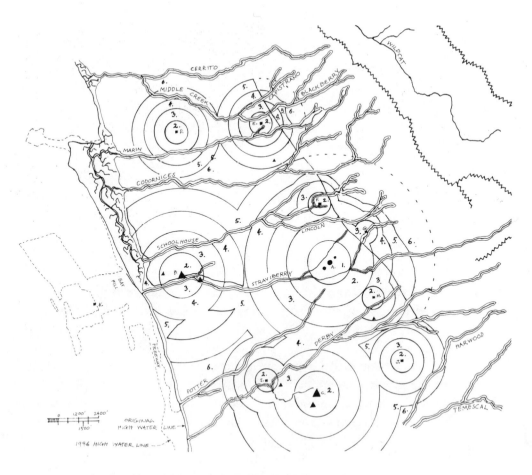

Map 2. ECOCITY ZONING GUIDE—
SELECTING CENTERS, MAPPING ECOCITY ZONES

idealized center of town	•	idealized sub-centers	▲
actual town center	•	actual sub-centers	▲
compromise town center	●	compromise sub-centers	▲
existing neighborhood centers	■		

A. Downtown	E. Solano, Colusa	I. Sacramento, Ashby
B. West Berkeley	F. North Shattuck	J. Elmwood
C. South Berkeley	G. North Campus	K. Marina
D. Albany	H. South Campus	

easy and pleasant to walk and bicycle. This pattern of "spots" of development is based on the size of the human body and the speed of walking. It contrasts sharply with "strip" (one-dimensional or linear development) and "sprawl" (two-dimensional or flat development) created by and for things that weigh 10 to 40 times as much and travel up to 50 times as fast: automobiles.

Draw the circles using the downtown, the major sub-centers and the neighborhood centers as centerpoints for the radii. For downtown and the two large sub-centers in West and South Berkeley use increments of 400 yards in drawing the circles (slightly less than 1/4 mile). For neighborhoods, a more intimate walking scale is called for—use 200 yard radii.

When circles are drawn, label the zones 1, 2, 3, 4, 5, and 6 as you move out from the centers. Future "proximity policies" will be based largely on these zones. The idea here is to give advantage to people closer to the centers since they have a far healthier impact upon nature, resources and vital cultural life than people far from centers.

Zone One will have the heaviest investment of positive incentives and subsidies and will encourage high density development. Zone six will have the heaviest disincentives for living or working in the area and will have strong positive incentives to move—unless the resident wants to work in food-growing, or land restoration and stewardship. The other zones grade off from one to the other, the outlying areas becoming less populated with time, the centers becoming more populated.

Next we need to adjust our circumferences in consideration of natural hazards and steep slopes. Slopes require more energy, technology, and expense to traverse than flat or gently sloped terrain. Hills are more car-dependent, less bicycle-accessible than flatter land, and more unstable for building. Where slopes are steep enough to discourage bicycling for everyday purposes, reduce the radii to one third. In the zones of natural hazard, shift the zone number to one higher, from 2 to 3, for example. This makes development less likely there but doesn't prohibit it—good technology can overcome most natural hazards, but it is expensive and should be somewhat discouraged and saved instead for places closer to the town centers. A lot of technology and craftsmanship now lavished on homes and landscaping of neighborhoods in zones five and six, including public-supported work on storm drainage, retaining walls, tree trimming, and road maintenance, should be lavished instead on public areas in-town and neighborhood centers.

In Map 2 we have drawn our Ecocity Zoning Guide which shows which land is to be favored by proximity policies. Over 20 or 30 years, land and property taxes are to be slowly raised in the high-number zones and lowered toward the centers. Employers, bankers, and home owners are urged to provide jobs, loans, and rental space to people partially on the basis of which zones they live in and how far they have to travel to work. Proximity, ignored in most such decision-making today, would be included among the many other considerations in such decision-making in the future.

Policies that shift incentives from sprawl to diverse centers, such as taxing according to the ecocity zoning guide, should be instituted over the long term so that people can adjust with the city infrastructure changes. When assistance programs of any sort are made available, say Section 8 housing money or state and federal development loans and grants, disaster relief, and so on, assistance should be apportioned more heavily per capita in the central zones.

Now we look at the city as it is, Map 3. Pay special attention to areas of high investment of human energy and capital such as downtown and University buildings and transit infrastructure. Note special historic places to be maintained and views to be developed in ways that celebrate the location. While protecting some views we shouldn't lose track of the fact that beautiful buildings *create* good views. We should recognize that even ugly buildings may provide work places and homes for many people grateful to have a job and a place to live. Locate the areas of least density and human investment—these are the places of highest potential for opening up agricultural and natural lands. And take note of railroad right of ways—don't *ever* build on them (though in many cases building *over* them is fine). Railroad right of ways usually connect higher density areas and could again make the best routes for streetcars, trains, or bicycles in a more energy- and ecology-aware future. The old Santa Fe right of way, now abandoned and donated to the city of Berkeley, is the local case in point.

From here on out we should pay special attention to what we might think of as the cultural endowment: the working-class heritage of the oldest part of town, the Oceanview neighborhood in West Berkeley; the presence of the University of California, one of the intellectual centers of the world; for better or worse, Berkeley's historic role in developing the atomic bomb (it was also the place where plutonium was first created); its role in the Free Speech and Peace Movement; its place as home of People's Park, which was expanded in 1980 when

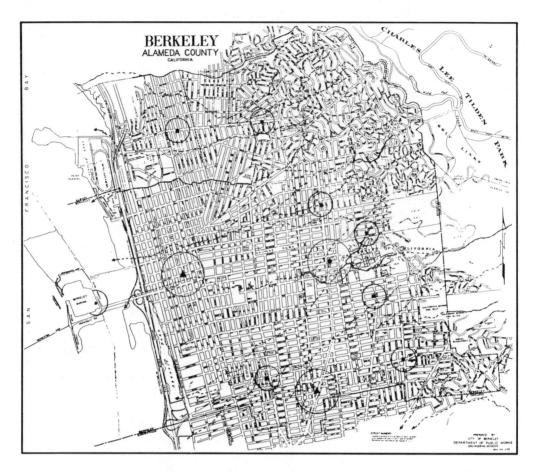

Map 3. BERKELEY AND ITS CENTERS

"street people" tore up a parking lot of 120 places and planted gardens; and its tradition of cultural and racial diversity. The Ecology Center (the first in the United States), Farallones Institute and Urban Ecology, Inc. have contributed to making Berkeley a leader in appropriate technology and city-planning innovation. The area is now well on its way to becoming the Silicon Valley of genetic engineering, which raises both positive and negative possibilities which everybody will eventually have to deal with. And though they are now almost completely forgotten, we would do well to remember the remarkable heritage of the Ohlone Indians, a people who, despite great linguistic differences among groups, lived in peace with one another—and with almost negligible impact on nature—here on this very land we Berkeleyans walk daily.

The name of the whole region, the San Francisco Bay Area, is a name with special significance as well. Saint Francis was the patron

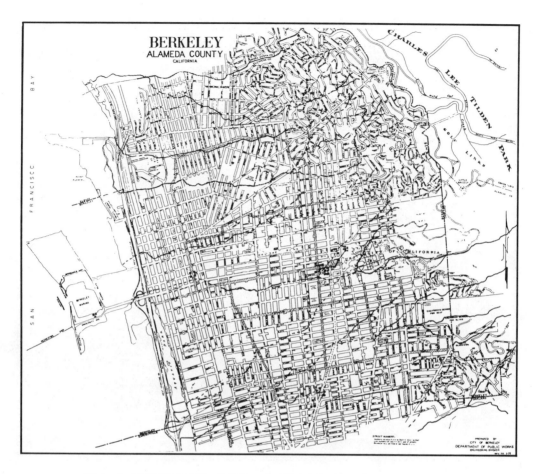

Map 4. BERKELEY, 5 TO 15 YEARS HENCE

saint of wildlife (as much as there was of "ecology" at the time), and
a legendary example of peacefulness. We would do well to remember
this heritage too when planning Berkeley's future.

In Map 4 we imagine changes facilitated by the Ecocity Zoning
Guide (Map 2), and with early stages of other city-wide and neighborhood projects such as creek restoration campaigns and street closings
in the lowest density areas.

The time is 5 to 15 years after Map 3, essentially "the present."

- A slow streets system is established (streets with crosshatching).
- Some new buildings and some old are being connected by pedestrian
  bridges in Downtown, the marina, and west and south centers (black
  shapes connected by short, thin lines).
- In the lowest-density areas some dilapidated and fire-damaged houses

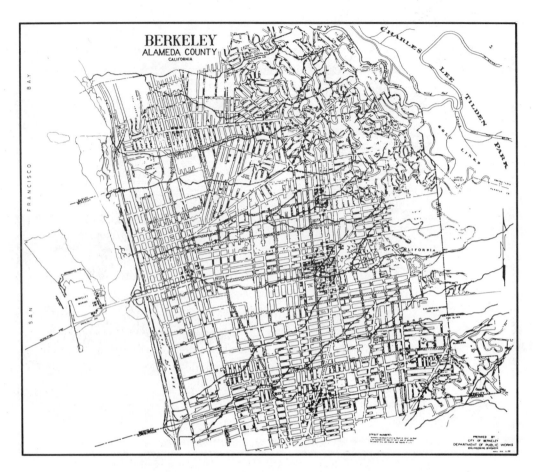

Map 5. BERKELEY, 15 TO 50 YEARS HENCE

are removed and not replaced; occasionally the least active streets
are closed to through traffic, turned into gardens at one end and
parking at the other; or in some cases, closed altogether to cars
and replaced by modest foot and bicycle paths.

- Large parts of the shoreline and long stretches of creeks are being
restored.

In Map 5 we imagine Berkeley in 15 to 50 years.

- More lower-density areas are opened up as some people take advantage of positive incentives to move closer to centers; many find
jobs and homes in close proximity; many also sell their cars. As
the contrast between disincentives in high-numbered zones and
incentives in low-numbered zones increases year by year, more people take the opportunity to move.

- Virtually all sections of Strawberry Creek and many stretches of the other creeks have been opened; fish return as runoff and pollution problems begin to abate.
- Streetcars return, connecting North Shattuck, Downtown, South Berkeley, and Oakland. North Berkeley BART Station is being downgraded as two thirds of its parking lot is removed for farming. Half the parking that remains is for bicycles and small electric cars—and serves six times as many people as the car parking lot.
- Many buildings are now connected by bridges and the downtown is connected to the School of Ecocity Design by a bicycle and foot bridge. Two or three buildings in downtown are now taller than the Great Western Building, and two or three in West and South Berkeley are taller than eight stories. They are linked by bridges and have rooftop public places—cafes, sculpture gardens, and promenades with panoramic views. Many of the larger buildings have solar greenhouses, rooftop gardens, wind-electric generators and other ecocity features. Serious money is now being invested in non-automobile transportation infrastructure and services; transfer of development rights goes on regularly and crossover funding is moving gas tax and car tax money into mixed-use development in centers.
- The Marina changes from a peninsula to an island to allow water circulation and create a strong unique community. Aquatic Park, formerly a slightly sad, very noisy, semi-stagnant body of water, is livened by a new connection with the Bay as the freeway is made to bridge the water in two places. Considerable development goes on at the marina, sponsored largely by the Santa Fe Land Company, turning it into a vital center with fishing, tourism, offices, homes—and Venice-like canals.

In Map 6 we imagine Berkeley in 25 to 90 years. Changes depicted in Map 5 are accentuated.

- Bicycle paths: small electric carts allowed at 15 miles per hour but no cars, buses, or trucks (except for essential delivery and emergency vehicles) are becoming common.
- North Berkeley BART Station is closed and Albany BART Station opened. Streetcars connect Albany and West Berkeley with Oakland and Richmond via San Pablo Blvd. and connect Downtown, West Berkeley and the Marina via University Avenue. Cable cars connect North Shattuck, Elmwood, and downtown with the

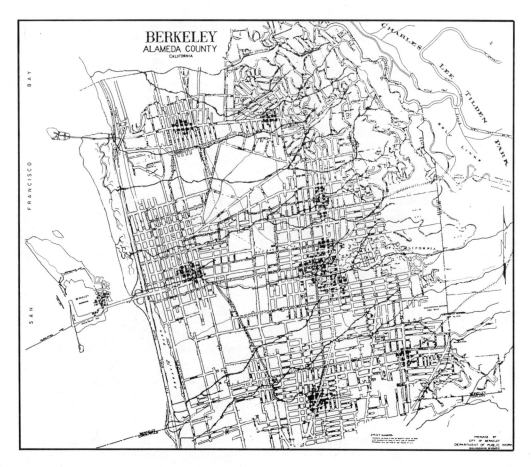

Map 6. BERKELEY, 25 TO 90 YEARS HENCE

spectacular views from the Berkeley Hills ridgeline.

- If we manage to survive another 25 or 90 years it will be because we are at least beginning to substitute an ecological-recovery economy for a war-based economy—which means large resources become available for the first time since the 30s for public works. One such would be the dredging of ill-conceived bay-fill to return healthy water circulation and restore marshes—which brings back enormous numbers of aquatic life and birds.
- The freeway fill is now gone and the four-lane freeway stands on pilings—the east shore of Aquatic Park is now the east shore of the Bay of San Francisco. A beach is being established here and people are beginning to talk of putting the freeway underground somewhere around Fourth Street.

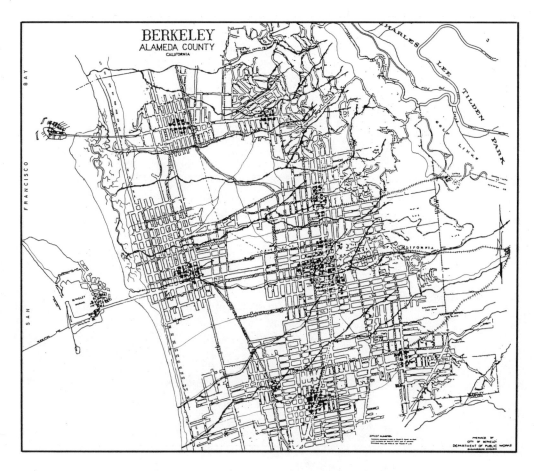

BERKELEY
ALAMEDA COUNTY
CALIFORNIA

Map 7. BERKELEY, 40 TO 125 YEARS HENCE

Map 7 represents a hypothetical Berkeley 40 to 125 years after Map 3.

- The freeway is placed underground. After more than a generation of Berkeley's ecocity influence—and deterioration of ecosphere and world resources—other communities are getting serious about ecocity land uses. Finally, as jobs, housing, recreation, and other activities are arranged closer together, freeway traffic slows to a trickle. Between cities at great distance, planes and trains handle almost all the traffic; between cities at moderate distances, mostly trains operate, with some buses and rental cars. A more sociable people, less addicted to TV, blessed with the gifts of conversation and story-telling, takes to the hills and beaches in groups; shared cars, vans, small buses, and small trains travel to resorts. Many people bicycle the network of tiny paved car-free roads which can take them thousands of miles through the country in a couple of weeks at almost no cost—and cyclists can reach out their hands and touch the passing trees, lay their bikes in the grass and listen to the slightest breeze. Try that on a freeway!

- As a four lane highway, the East Shore Freeway is reasonably scaled to be placed underground. In the vicinity of cities it looks from above like a line of skylights marching through orchards a block or so from the railroad tracks. In West Berkeley there are four or five vent/filters: concrete boxes fifteen feet high with colorful murals on their sides.
- Small resort communities appear at the heads of the cable car lines—interlinked buildings at the state of the art in solar, wind, and biodynamic architecture.
- Nature thrives and agriculture is more bountiful than ever in Berkeley's early history.
- 150,000 people are living on 65% of the land inhabited by 100,000 in the 1980s.
- The city recycles 85% of its waste flow and consumes one third the energy consumed in the 1980s.

A striking feature in comparing Berkeley of the 1980s (Map 3) with ecocity Berkeley (Map 7): the texture of the later map creates the impression that your vantage point has risen three or four times higher into the sky so that you are now looking down into a whole region with cities, open country, highways connecting. If we lower our vantage point to one-third or one-quarter the height of our perspective on all these maps, however, we don't find (in the last map) the relative uniformity we'd discover in the map of Berkeley in the 1980s. Instead of finding, for example, flat, uniform residential densities stretching for six or seven blocks in every direction, or an industrial zone, or a downtown of office buildings, we'd discover in each of these areas a great deal more, much of it natural or agricultural. At this scale we would also be able to see individual people moving about—they are all within a short walk of tremendous variety. Thus we would have achieved a genuine human scale for a rich cultural/natural, urban/country texture of living.

WHAT OF THE DEEPER FUTURE?

It's assuming a lot to hope that humanity might conquer fear of itself and end the insane violence and preparations for war that seek to "defend" one group from another. Proclaiming peace with nature and starting off toward ecocity building would at least ease ourselves toward a state of mind and heart that substitutes creation for destruction, stewardship for fearful hoarding. If we do pull back from the brink and reinvest in a healthy future, reinvest all that capital, technology, and genius now placed in the service of fear and hate, we could assure not only all the changes described here in this book but many unforeseen changes and improvements.

In Berkeley's case, for example, large ecological, aesthetic public works could include the removal of millions of tons of fill dumped into the Bay to support the freeway. Where would the fill go? It could become an artificial mountain, like Mount Trashmore near Chicago, on which people ski every winter. However, this mountain could be much larger, built from the un-recyclable waste of several cities, rising from the back slopes of the Berkeley Hills, creating extraordinary views. Solar electric and methane trucks would deliver the fill. Local climates would diversify slightly as the urban volcano rises layer by layer. Snow would fall occasionally on Mount Tamalpais, Mount Diablo, and Mount Orinda.

Today, many people remodel their houses as a matter of course, making them more enjoyable: a skylight here, a greenhouse there. In the future, big old boring buildings could be remodeled too, with deep light shafts angling several stories down into the interiors bringing winter sun into multi-storied, terraced courtyards. New steel could be added for support—as it is now done for earthquake protection.

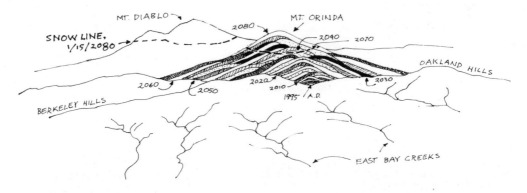

URBAN VOLCANO

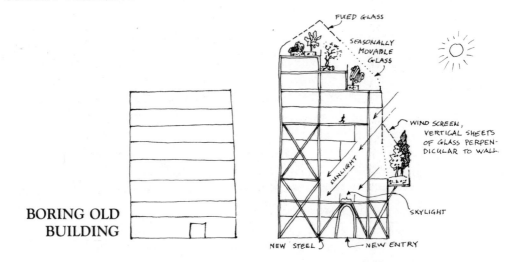

BORING OLD BUILDING

REMODELED

SCISSOR LIFT AND CHERRY PICKER TOURS

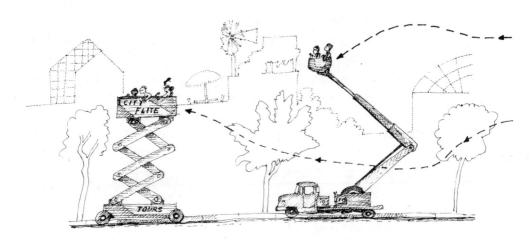

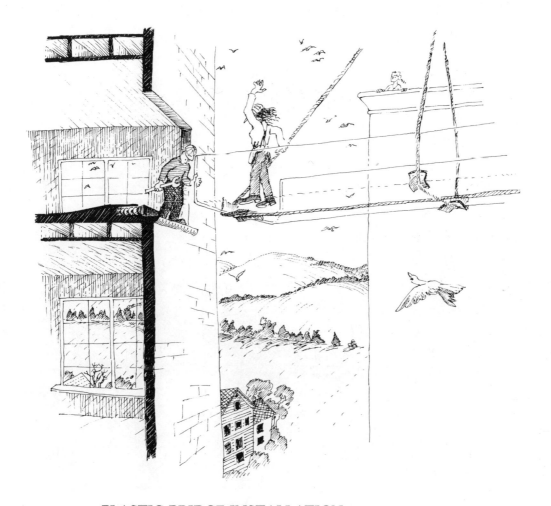

PLASTIC BRIDGE INSTALLATION

Today we burn small lakes and mountains of oil and coal every day. In the ecocity future we could use the same resources for advanced structural plastics—single member extruded transparent bridges, for example. These would be expensive to manufacture but simple and relatively inexpensive to install. Oversized shock absorbers at each end would help brace buildings against earthquake damage.

If we radically reduce street congestion we might discover an enterprising tour company or two offering rides through town on scissor lifts or "cherry pickers". Such tours would recall the sense of flying in dreams, looking down, with the birds, into the trees, gliding over landscapes and streets, familiar or completely new. These rides would pro-

---

ECOCITY IN A BERKELEY-LIKE ENVIRONMENT

vide an exciting new perspective—literally—on our urban life and would be especially delightful for children.

And the city and its neighborhoods? They would be gleaming gems set in the garden we forsook hundreds of years ago only to recreate. They would be an artform in which we all participate called building and living the ecocity.

One or two hundred years ago, if anyone had projected an image of the Bay Area—or any urban area—as it actually is today, it would have earned derision for the seer, derision for what has become a reality. Radical change will occur, guided or not. So it serves realism to keep an open mind about the possibilities. It also serves our survival and destiny as a creative, compassionate species.

WHEN WILL WE
HAVE AN ECOCITY?

No one will ever agree on when we will have an ecocity because ecocities are a direction, not a destination. No city stands still. They are
each a dynamic dance of stone, wood, flesh, and shimmering energy
flows, an interplay of the ancient forces of nature and history upon
the volatile spirit of humanity, hopefully volatile in the future in a
more creative and less destructive way than the way in which we have
become accustomed.

    If one day we have a space-age downtown of tall buildings with

---

school kids fishing in the creek, with speedy streetcars zipping between centers, and lazy bicyclists floating across open fields from one orchard-lined neighborhood to another neighborhood gathered up into a redwood canyon, we will be pretty far along. If the air is clean at last and the creeks are running full and fresh, if the people are eating healthy local food, getting lots of exercise, both physical and mental, and if the people are sighting animals, birds, fish and plants gone for the last fifty or one hundred years, we will have accomplished a lot.

But once we have started seeking the healthiest, most vital relationship of city to nature, we will discover there is no end to it in time or variety. The journey is infinitely long, but its goal will arrive over and over in infinite forms along the way, emerging from the interplay of our own creativity and nature's regenerative abundance. We will never *solve* all our problems, but once we launch this journey, we will at least *be solving* them from then on.

RESOURCES: INTERNATIONAL
AND GENERAL

Arcosanti, Arizona 86333. Construction project and small communi‑
ty aspiring to build a high-density, single-structure town on natural
and agricultural land.

Auroville, Kottakuppam 605104, Tamil Nadu, India. Spiritual/human‑
istic/international community seeking to build a city of peace in
harmony with nature.

Cerro Gordo, Box 569, Cottage Grove, Oregon 97424. Planning and
building a village-scale ecologically healthy and sustainable com‑
munity. Family and cooperative values emphasized.

New Alchemy Institute, 237 Hatchville Rd. East, Falmouth, Massa‑
chusetts 02536. Innovators of biotechnologies in aquaculture and
small-scale high-intensity farming, builders of solar structures, wind
and solar energy systems, with research and publications.

Permaculture Institute, Box 96, Stanley, Tasmania 7331, Australia,
or Permaculture Institute of North America, 6488 Maxwell Road,
Clinton, Washington 98507. Designing and implementing sustain‑
able rural and urban ecosystems with an agricultural focus, some
architectural emphasis, and a little attention to urban design.

Planet Drum, Box 31251, San Francisco, California 94131. Broad‑
ranging bioregional specifics artistically portrayed, leading to polit‑
ical, cultural and ecological action around the world.

Regeneration Project, Rodale Press, 33 Minor St., Emmas, Pennsylvania
18049. Helps organize economic, cooperative, small community
and small business projects. Publishes success stories and helps in
networking.

Trust for Public Land, 82 2nd St., San Francisco, California 94105.
Land Banking for rural and urban open and public spaces for gar‑
dening and cultural purposes.

Urban Ecology, 1939 Cedar St., Berkeley, California 94709. Works
on theory and practice of ecocity-building, publishing ideas and
news while implementing projects in Berkeley. Presently (but pos‑
sibly not permanently) inactive—contact only for publications listed
under "Readings, International and General."

READINGS: INTERNATIONAL AND GENERAL

A Landscape for Humans, Peter Van Dresser, The Lightning Tree, Santa Fe, 1972.

A Pattern Language, Christopher Alexander, Oxford University Press, New York, 1977.

Arcology—The City in the Image of Man, Paolo Soleri, MIT Press, Cambridge, Massachusetts, 1969.

Bioshelters, Ocean Arks, City Farming: Ecology as the Basis of Design, Nancy Jack Todd and John Todd, Sierra Club Books, San Francisco, 1984.

Cities and the Wealth of Nations, Jane Jacobs, Random House, New York, 1985.

Compact Cities: Energy Saving Strategies for the Eighties, Subcommittee on the City, Committee on Banking, Finance and Urban Affairs, U.S. House of Representatives, U.S. Government Printing Office, Washington, 1980.

The Cost of Sprawl, Real Estate Research Corporation, prepared for HUD, EPA and the Council on Environmental Quality, U.S. Government Printing Office, Washington, 1980.

Creating Alternative Futures, Hazel Henderson, Berkeley Windhover, New York, 1978.

Design With Nature, Ian McHarg, Doubleday/Natural History Press, Philadelphia, 1969.

The Edible City, Richard Britz, William Kaufman, Los Altos, California, 1979.

Gaia, An Atlas of Planet Management, Norman Myers Gaia Books Limited and Anchor Books, Garden City, New York, 1984.

Healthy Harvest—A Directory of Sustainable Agriculture and Horticulture Organizations, Susan J. Sanzone, Ed., Potomac Valley Press, Washington, D.C. 1987.

Mixed Uses, A Design and Zoning Proposal for Davis, California (largely implemented), Lois H. Scott, City of Davis, Davis, 1977.

Permaculture I and *Permaculture II*, Bill Mollison and David Holmgren, Tagari, Stanley, Tasmania, 1978 and 1979.

Seeds for Change, Deborah White et. al, Patchwork Press, North Melbourne, Australia, 1978.

Sustainable Communities, Sim Van der Ryn and Peter Calthorpe, Eds.,

Sierra Club Books, New York, 1984.

"In Context" (magazine), Sustainable Habitat Issue, #14, Autumn, 1986, P.O. Box 2107, Sequim, Washington 98382.

"Planning and Constructing Integral Neighborhoods," a conference proceedings by Urban Ecology, Inc., Berkeley, 1979, $5.00, 1939 Cedar St., Berkeley California 94709.

"The Urban Ecologist" (newsletter), Tenth Anniversary Issue, Urban Ecology, Inc., Berkeley, California, 1986, $5.00, same address.

RESOURCES: BERKELEY AND ITS BIOREGION

Berkeley City Government: The following are directly related to ecocity ideas and projects and should be sympathetic (eventually if not already): The Mayor's Office, Housing and Economic Development Offices, Planning, Parks and Recreation, Transportation, Art, and Energy Commissions, 2180 Milvia Street, Berkeley, CA 94704.

East Bay Bicycle Coalition, P. O. Box 1736, Oakland, CA 94618. General advocates for bicycle transportation for sport, pleasure and utility.

Ecology Center, 1403 Addison St., Berkeley, CA 94704. Helps with networking and education for local action and runs the local curbside recycling program.

Green City (a project of Planet Drum Foundation), Box 31251, San Francisco, CA 94131. An attempt to develop a popularly supported ecologically healthy plan for San Francisco.

People for Open Space, 512 Second Street, San Francisco, CA 94107. Protecting the Bay Area's greenbelt and open space, promoting compact/diverse centers, opposing sprawl.

Sierra Club San Francisco Bay Chapter, 6014 College Ave., Oakland, CA 94618. Wide ranging ecocity-type support in land use, transportation, energy, pollution and open space issues.

Urban Creeks Council, 2634 Grant Street, Berkeley, CA 94703. Promotes creek restoration and preservation, educates on the subject and takes political action, mainly in the East Bay.

READINGS: BERKELEY
AND ITS BIOREGION

Ecotopia. Ernest Callenbach, Banyan Tree, Berkeley, 1975.

The Integral Urban House, Farallones Institute, Sierra Club Books, San Francisco, 1979.

The Ohlone Way, Malcolm Margolin, Heyday Books, Berkeley, 1978.

Weather of the San Francisco Bay Area, Harold Gilliam, University of California Press, Berkeley, 1962.

"*The Ecology Center Newsletter*," Berkeley, above address.

Planet Drum publications, called "bundles," San Francisco, above address; their Green Cities publication is especially interesting.

"*The Yodeler*," newsletter of the Sierra Club San Francisco Bay Chapter, Oakland, above address.

Urban Ecology publications, see page 137.

Outline

I Intro
   · What is sustainable development
   · Cities and their problems
   · How does sustainable development tie in w/ cities
   · History of ecocities

II Background on the cities
                        · Berkeley

III Planning

IV Architecture

V Policy

VI Citizen action